D1476509

TYING TROUT FLIES

BY C. BOYD PFEIFFER

Published by

**krause
publications**

700 East State Street • Iola, WI 54990-0001
715/445-2214 • FAX: 715/445-4087   www.krause.com

Please call or write for our free catalog of publications.
Our toll-free number to place an order or obtain a free catalog is
(800) 258-0929.

Library of Congress Catalog Number: 2001096281
ISBN: 0-87349-292-7

Dedication

To Brenda

Acknowledgments

It all started when I was about 12. An old bachelor who lived next door gave me a fly-tying outfit so I could tie some trout flies. He liked to teach boys fishing, and was a mentor of many boys before me. He died about six years later when in his mid-60s. Before his death, he taught me about all types of fishing, made sure that I got good tackle and tied flies for me until providing me with the above-mentioned fly-tying kit. That fishing and fly-tying instruction was important to me, since no one – no one – in my family had any interest in the sport that I had learned to love.

After some first crude attempts, I began to get better at tying all types of trout flies. Ultimately, I began tying flies for everything from bass and bluegills to saltwater stripers and sharks, and eventually flies for bonefish, tarpon, permit, pike, carp, steelhead, shad, and billfish – you name it. Along the way, I learned from others by both reading books on fly-tying and watching the skills of those better and more experienced than I – something that continues to this day.

Friends – most of whom tie flies – also helped, even though they perhaps did not know it at the time. Close friends then and now, such as Chuck Edghill, Lefty Kreh, Ed Russell, Norm Bartlett, Joe Zimmer, Irv Swope, Bill May, Jim Heim and others have served as both sounding boards for some crazy ideas and also mentors and instructors in fly-tying techniques.

I also appreciate the help of friends in the industry who provided advice, help, or flies for inclusion in the book and for photos. These include: John Mazurkiewicz of Catalyst Marketing, Bill Black of Spirit River, Rainy Riding of Rainy Riding Flies, Phil Camera of InterTac, McKenzie Flies, Spirit River, Umpqua, Brookside Flies, Riverborn Flies, Joe Messinger, Jr., Pacific Fly Group, Holly Flies, Brookside Flies, Rod Yerger, and others.

My longtime fishing companion and close friend Chuck Edghill deserves special mention and thanks. He tied many of the flies used in the book and also served as consultant to the book content. In addition, as he has done with past books, he read the manuscript to correct typos, spelling mistakes, grammar, and in general added his wisdom to the book to make it better than it would have been without his thoughtful advice. Naturally, any errors and faults that remain are mine, and my responsibility, but this is a better book because of Chuck Edghill. In addition, I thank my wife Brenda for allowing me, shortly after our marriage, the time to complete the book. Finally, my thanks for the patience and interest by Don Gulbrandsen, Kevin Michalowski and others at Krause Publications for extending the deadline and being patient with me during this project.

C. Boyd Pfeiffer
October 2001

Table of Contents

About the Photographs

Trout flies are typically small, but for photo clairty and reader understandability, most of the "methods" photos were taken using oversize hooks. In all cases, proportions were kept appropriate for the hook size. In most cases, only materials necessary for describing and showing the method were included in each photo, even though fly-tying involves progressively adding materials to complete a given fly.

In addition, contrasting materials were used, again for photo clarity. For example, many trout flies use a thread color matching or complimentary to the body. In all cases, thread and other material colors were chosen for contrast so that the step or methods illustrated would be as clear as possible to the reader.

Foreword

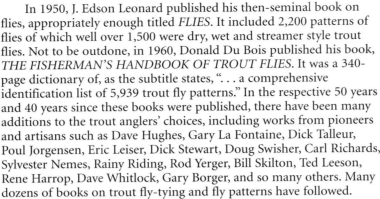

In 1950, J. Edson Leonard published his then-seminal book on flies, appropriately enough titled *FLIES*. It included 2,200 patterns of flies of which well over 1,500 were dry, wet and streamer style trout flies. Not to be outdone, in 1960, Donald Du Bois published his book, *THE FISHERMAN'S HANDBOOK OF TROUT FLIES*. It was a 340-page dictionary of, as the subtitle states, ". . . a comprehensive identification list of 5,939 trout fly patterns." In the respective 50 years and 40 years since these books were published, there have been many additions to the trout anglers' choices, including works from pioneers and artisans such as Dave Hughes, Gary La Fontaine, Dick Talleur, Poul Jorgensen, Eric Leiser, Dick Stewart, Doug Swisher, Carl Richards, Sylvester Nemes, Rainy Riding, Rod Yerger, Bill Skilton, Ted Leeson, Rene Harrop, Dave Whitlock, Gary Borger, and so many others. Many dozens of books on trout fly-tying and fly patterns have followed.

In addition, there has been an explosion of available synthetic materials, often occurring concurrently as, unfortunately, some of the natural furs and feathers became unavailable. The loss of these feathers and furs as a result of species becoming rare and endangered is tragic, and another story.

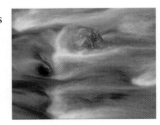

The new synthetic materials, along with a renewed interest in trout fishing and fly-tying, occurred perhaps in part as a result of organizations such as Trout Unlimited and the Federation of Fly Fishers, and the various fly-tying conclaves and symposiums held throughout the country. In addition, there is now a greater understanding of the life cycles of mayflies, caddis, stoneflies, and the other lesser-known aquatic insects. This has in turn brought about innovation in design of trout flies by some of the most imaginative people in the business. The result is a wealth of new patterns and new thoughts on flies for trout, along with a blurring of the categories into which we placed trout flies years ago.

Up through the 1950s, you could categorize trout flies into dry flies, wet flies, nymphs, and streamers. Some who tie flies separated streamers further into "bucktails" tied with a hair wing, and "streamers" tied with a feather wing. Dry flies were then usually the Catskill-style dries, perky trim flies designed ideally to float on hackle tips and tails. Wet flies were most often tied with a standard throat hackle or collar hackle and a quill wing. Nymphs were simple, and often not separated into the various species of insect or some of the highly imitative designs that are available today. Streamers and bucktails could be complex, but always had a body wrapped on the hook shank and a wing on top.

Today, Woolly Buggers, Zonkers and Matukas are added to the streamer category; leeches have been added to the general arsenal; and soft-hackle wet flies as per the original ties of 500 years ago and the more recent developments of sparse, soft-hackle patterns have been re-discovered by Nemes and others. Nymphs have gained great importance in fly boxes. Emergers (nymphs appearing on the surface to shuck their larval case) and emergers and duns with a trailing shuck (the case left from their metamorphosis) have all become important. Other additions are duns that float on and in the surface film as per the naturals (Comparaduns and Sparkle Duns with a trailing shuck), and spinners with transparent poly film wings. A river of articles and some books and videos have become available on the importance of the diminutive species such as Tricos, Caenis and Baetis species.

As a result of all this, innovators have developed entire families of flies and specific designs based on their concepts of what trout like to eat. Thus, you can find flies tied by different people, all imitations of the same species of a nymph and all of which will be markedly different imitations. The same applies to mayfly emergers, duns, and spinners, as well as baitfish, leeches, caddis, stoneflies, crane flies, and terrestrials such as ants, jassids, hoppers, crickets, beetles, inchworms, and caterpillars.

For the beginner this presents a wealth of diversity and innovative thought as to trout fly design, but also a blurring of the boundaries of the past. Do you put a floating nymph into the dry fly category or the nymph category? Is a Sparkle Dun or Comparadun a true dry? Is a simple Gray Nymph really a nymph or more like a wet fly? Where do you put a Leech or a Woolly Bugger? My answers, respectively, would be nymph, a true dry, I'm not sure, and I don't know. What's more, I don't care.

These new fields of fly-tying should not discourage anyone with different answers than mine or strong feelings about the above. Nor, in my view, should we be greatly concerned about into which category we should fit a particular fly. The broadening of categories, the expansion of ideas only gives us more flies with more diversity and in a word, more ammunition with which to challenge trout.

Naturally, the enclosed list of 100 top patterns will no doubt engender thought, some controversy, and even some disagreement. Note that it is not the "top 100 flies" since that would suggest that any other flies are not worthy of this listing of 100 patterns. Each fly on the enclosed list is designed to show a particular tying style or an example of a fly that will work in all parts of the country or perhaps be specific to a certain area of the country. Some flies are ideal for working long glides; others for working rough runs or pocket water; some for lakes and still-water streams. Some are Eastern flies for the smaller streams in which pools alternate with riffles. Some are Western flies for the often larger, rougher faster waters found there. In short, no fly will do everything all the time, or on all waters, or even necessarily all day long. That's the challenge of trout fishing and of tying trout flies.

Realize that many of the designs here may also differ slightly from the same "pattern" that you see in other books, particularly older books on fly-tying. The development of synthetics and the loss of some natural materials requires this, while many who tie flies have developed their own slight variations of standard classic patterns. In different references, I've found slight variations in the wing design of a Mickey Finn streamer; in the wings, tails and hackles of many dry flies; in the materials of many nymphs; in the use of dubbing (natural or blended synthetic) or body material (stranded dubbing such as Gudebrod E-Z Dub, Leech Yarn, mohair) in some dries, wet flies and nymphs.

That is part of the pleasure of fly-tying. You can go back to the originals and tie the exact pattern as developed by earlier experts such as Harry Darbee, Art Flick, Preston Jennings, Vince Marinaro, Charlie Fox, Theodore Gordon, Jim Leisenring and others. You can tie examples from the masters of today such as Poul Jorgensen, Dick Talleur, Bill Hunter, Gary Borger, Dave Hughes, Gary La Fontaine, and so many others. You can go out on your own to modify existing patterns slightly – changing a material, color, proportion (note the variant dries, tied with extremely oversize tails and hackles) - or modify the profile or silhouette of a fly from that of previous patterns. Or, you can just play with materials to come up with something radically new and different and perhaps extremely effective. The basics are here to play with in this book through coverage of popular flies and the various tying methods used to construct a fly of any type.

Once you know the basics, it is just a matter of practice, imagination and innovation. After all, reduced to its elements, fly-tying is all pretty much just securing a string on a hook, and tying stuff down on it to make something attractive to fish.

Chapter 1

Essential Tools and Accessory Tools

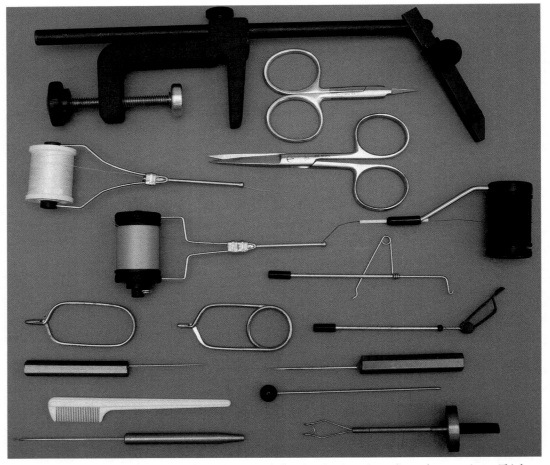

Tools for fly tying. These include, left to right: top row; simple fly-tying vise. Second row, fine and coarse scissors. Third row; standard bobbin, Griffin adjustable-tension bobbin and Merco adjustable-tension bobbin. Fourth row; two types of standard hackle pliers, Griffin rotating hackle pliers and whip finisher. Fifth row; two bodkins. Sixth row; comb and bobbin cleaner. Seventh row; bobbin threader and dubbing loop tool.

Essential Tools

While it might be possible to tie flies with no tools at all, it would be ill-advised. You could hold the hook with one hand, wrap the thread with your fingers (no bobbin), wrap hackle with your fingers, and cut the thread with a pocketknife. The tying process would not be fun; the result might not be pretty. Good tools – they need not be expensive – are a must to get started right in tying flies. You need only the essentials to get started – any accessory or additional tools can be added as desired or needed.

Essential tools include the following:

VISE – A good fly-tying vise is a necessity. This does not mean that it has to be expensive. Some very good reasonably priced vises are available. Basic vise choices include rotary or stationary, the method of jaw closure and the type of base. True rotary styles allow turning the vise jaws by means or a crank or knob. The hook shank stays on the axis of the rotation to allow adding materials by feeding the material to the turning hook. Those vises that allow turning of the hook in which the hook does not stay horizontal allow some tying adjustments, but are not true rotary. The true rotary vises are best if you start tying commercially or are tying a lot of large flies in which a lot of wrapped body material is added.

Traditional vise jaws close by a cam system in which the jaws are pulled back against a collet at the end of a sleeve to tighten the jaws on the hook. The jaws are pulled back by means of a cam operated by a lever positioned at the end of the sleeve or barrel. Some modern vises close using a pivotal thumbscrew system that levers the jaws together to hold the hook.Both systems work well, and both systems allow for jaw adjustment to hold a large range of hook sizes. The hook size range will vary with the vise manufacturer. Some vises have interchangeable jaws, with fine pointed jaw tips for holding very small trout hooks and larger, more blunt jaws for holding large hooks used for warm-water or saltwater, or when tying any large flies.

Basic vise types for all of the above include the "C" clamp style and pedestal style. The "C" clamp style is just what it sounds like – a "C" clamp fastens the vise post to a table or bench. The advantage is that it is very stable and solid, but must have a table of the right thickness to clamp securely. An additional thumbscrew adjustment on the "C" clamp allows vertically positioning of the vise. The pedestal style usually has a shorter post holding the jaws and fits into a heavy pedestal. It has the advantage of being able to be positioned anywhere on a table or bench, and does not depend upon table style or thickness. The pedestal has the advantage of being useful in any situation, such as for travel or tying in a motel room, although the weight of the base makes this a disadvantage for air travel. Both of these styles work well. Most of these vises allow you to change between "C" clamp and pedestal base.

Manufacturers that make true rotary and rotary-style vises include Norlander, Renzetti, Dyna-King, Griffin, B's Fly Fishing Products, Abel, Anvil, HMH, Regal, D.H. Thompson, and others. Those that make vises with interchangeable jaws include HMH and Thompson.

LIGHT – Adequate light is a necessity for tying any fly. Light can vary from the simple 60-watt standard gooseneck to special desk lamps, to halogen lamps that provide intense light in a small area, to special color-corrected lamps that will show colors as they are in natural light (5,000 Kelvin color temperature). My favorites are the small halogen lights. These are available in stand-alone models from fly shops and general stores. Specialty models that clamp onto the vise post such as the models from McKenzie are also available. Just make sure that any lamp stands high enough above the vise jaws to give you good clearance for all wrapping and tying operations and is not too hot to work around.

BACKGROUND PLATE – A background contrasting with the fly color helps in seeing the materials and improves the end result. I like white for dark flies and black for light-colored flies, but I also switch to other colors just for a change of pace when doing a lot of tying. A Profile Plate from Dyna-King will fasten to any vise post, and comes with five color plates for varied flies. Lacking this, you can set up matte finish blotter paper at an angle in back of your vise.

HACKLE PLIERS – Hackle pliers are another necessity. They are designed to hold hackle while winding it around a hook, either when making a collar-style hackle for wet or dry flies, or when palmering the hackle over the body. Several styles are available. The most recent of these styles is a rotary type, with the small spring clamp fixed to a universal joint on the end of a thin handle. This allows holding the handle and winding the hackle, without changing the hackle pliers' position with each turn. This helps prevent twisting the hackle. I like this style best for most of my tying.

A more traditional design is the standard, or English style, that is made of spring steel bent so that two opposing jaws formed on the ends of the spring wire clamp together to grip the hackle. These are also made in a flat steel style with rubber buttons on one or both inside ends of the jaws to better grip the hackle. TIP – On any hackle pliers lacking soft jaws, it is easy to add a short length of thin surgical tubing, or a short length of shrink tubing, heated to hold it in place.

SCISSORS – Get good fly-tying scissors. Those with fine tips available from drug and cosmetics stores are generally not of good enough quality or have small finger holes that will not fit the average man. Also, buy two pairs of scissors. One pair must have very short fine tips that are ideal for cutting hackle and thread only and for fine work on the fly. The other pair should be larger, with tips about one to one and one-half inches long. Use these for any coarse cutting of lead wire, tinsels, metals, coarse thread and any mono or Kevlar thread. I prefer my scissors with one serrated jaw for better gripping and less slipping of materials being cut.

Some new scissors are available with tungsten or ceramic blades that will not dull under normal use. While they will not dull, both materials are very brittle. Use extreme care not to drop them or damage them, since they are far more expensive than the standard metal scissors.

BOBBIN – While you don't really need a bobbin, it does make it far easier to precisely position thread on a fly when adding materials and wrapping thread. It also makes it easier to control thread tension. Originally, they were only available in straight metal tube styles. Today, the best bobbins have a full ceramic tube, or a small ceramic ring (like a guide ring) fitted into the end of the tube through which the thread passes. Even though these are more expensive, they are well worth it. The straight metal tube bobbins will groove in time and damage thread. Avoid them. Bobbins are also available in short- and long-tube styles. You won't need a long-tube style for most trout flies, but if you later plan to tie large flies, any flies for warmwater or saltwater fly fishing, or any bugs or sliders, get one with a long tube. The long tube will be an advantage for larger flies where a greater bobbin "reach" is required.

One new bobbin by Griffin has an adjustable tension control on the spool holder. Similar bobbins with adjustable tension control are available from Norlander and Merco/Rite Bobbins.

BODKIN – Bodkins are basically needles on the end of a thin handle. They are useful for adding head cement to a finished fly, glue to fly parts, separating out hackle tips bound down by thread, pulling whip finishes up neatly, and many other tasks. You can buy them from any fly shop or catalog, or make them yourself. To make them, use pliers to carefully force the dull end of a needle into a wood dowel handle. Use different size needles for different purposes. Fine needles are good for separating out hackle and working on fine flies; coarser points are good for mixing glue and applying head cement.

HALF HITCH TOOL – Half hitch tools are nothing more than small tapered tools (like a pencil point with a hole where the pencil lead would be). To use one, loop the thread around the tool and hold the hole against the hook eye to slide the looped thread from the tool and onto the fly head to create a locking hitch on the fly head. Some half hitch tools have very deep holes so that the tool can be slipped over the hook eye and shank to place half hitches when tying down each material in turn. Half hitches are not as good as a whip finish, but are handy to temporarily lock thread. A whip finish should be used to complete each fly.

Accessory Tools

The following are tools that are very handy, but necessary only if you are tying flies that require their use. If you are never going to tie parachute-style dry flies, then you will never need a gallows tool. If you are always going to use head cement or nail polish and never add epoxy to the head of the fly, then you will not need a fly turner. If you will never make dubbed bodies using a thread loop, then you will not need a spinner or twister. If you can make a whip finish with your fingers, you will not need a whip finisher. The list goes on. Here then, are some suggestions of additional tools, but tools that should be added only after you make your initial selection of basic tools, mastered the basics of fly-tying and decided you have to have one of these tools.

TOOL RACK – Many of the vise and equipment manufacturers make various racks of wood, foam or plastic for holding fly-tying tools (bobbins, scissors, bodkins, hackle pliers) along with bottles of head cement, hair stackers, glues, marking pens, etc. Some racks for thread and other supplies are available from craft and sewing supply stores. You can make your own tool holder for scissors, bobbins and the like by drilling out a block of wood with the appropriate size holes, or cutting holes in a block of craft foam.

HACKLE AND PROPORTION GAUGE – There are several hackle and fly proportion gauges on the market. They are ideal for beginners or those who wish to be exact in their fly proportions. Gauges are all based on previously determined standard measurements. Some are designed to fit onto the vise post, others to be used freehand. Some measure just the radius of the hackle for each hook size, while others measure and give the proper proportions for dry fly wings, dry fly tails, streamers wings, etc. You will use one less and less as you tie, but initially they are well worth the small price.

BOBBIN THREADER – Bobbin threaders are made to help pull the thread through the bobbin tube. Some are a hard looped wire; others are a straight pin with a small hook or latchhook on the end. Considering that most bobbins, in time, get clogged with wax from the thread, these are a great help when changing threads. Consider also a bobbin cleaner to aid thread flow through the tube.

BOBBIN CLEANER – Bobbin cleaners are nothing more than a rod by which to push accumulated wax out of a bobbin tube. They are available commercially, but you can make one from a length of plastic rod that will fit easily into the bobbin tube. A short length of heavy monofilament from a Weed Wacker tool works fine for this.

WHIP FINISHER – Whip finishers are mechanical tools that allow easy rotation of the thread around the head of the fly to make the whip finish to tie off the thread. There are several different principles of use involved, depending on the brand that you purchase. All work well. Some allow positioning a whip finish only at the head of the fly while the well-known Matarelli allows placing a whip finish anywhere on the fly. This is not particularly important in trout flies, but can be important if you plan to tie warmwater or saltwater patterns. An alternative to this is to learn to make a whip finish with your fingers, although with small trout patterns this can be difficult when you also have to hold the hackle back and out of the way.

COMB – Fine-tooth combs are a must for removing the underfur from wing material such as deer hair, bucktail, and other fur where you want only the long guard hairs. Special combs for this are sold, but you can use any small comb. Possibilities are those used for combing mustaches and those used by women for combing eyelashes and eyebrows.

GALLOWS TOOL – These tools are designed to hold vertical the post for a parachute hackle while wrapping the hackle on parachute dry flies. As such, they are an aid when tying these flies. They can be homemade, but several styles – both simple and complex – are available commercially. Unless you plan to tie a lot of parachute dry flies, consider carefully before buying one of these, or make your own from hackle pliers and some light spring steel fastened to the vise post and angled over the fly, as per author Dick Talleur's idea.

WING BURNERS/WING CUTTERS – Wing burners are just what they sound like. They are specialized tweezers that allow you to center a quill (feather) between the burner jaws and, with a flame, burn away the exposed part of the feather to leave a simulation of a wing. They will make wings for mayflies, caddis and stoneflies. They are available commercially or you can make your own from thin brass or aluminum stock available at most hobby shops, hardware stores and some home handyman discount outlets. They are not used a great deal today.

Wing cutters are available again (there used to be a "rocking" style that would cut wings) with sets designed for various sizes of wings for mayflies, caddis flies, stone flies and hoppers. They will cut wings from feathers or from the synthetic sheets uses for such wings.

DUBBING TEASER – These tools are designed to tease out or slightly fray dubbing materials to make the body of a fly – usually a nymph – more buggy and suggestive of the natural insect. Most available commercially are similar to the small wire rasps used by dentists for root canal work. You can also make your own using a Popsicle stick to which is glued a section of the hook side of hook-and-loop (Velcro) fastener material.

DUBBING SPINNER – One way of adding dubbing to a fly is to bind it into a spun thread loop before wrapping it around the hook shank to form the body. Dubbing spinners allow twisting the thread loop to accomplish this. The same thing can be done with a hackle plier or the similar electronic grips or weighted heat sinks. Dubbing twisters come in simple hook style (like an open screw eye on a weighted handle) or wire loop style that holds the thread loop slightly open.

FLY TURNER – If tying streamer flies for trout, an epoxy finish on the head will often be quicker to add than multiple coats of head cement or clear nail polish. For this, you will need a slow-turning motor mounted with a plate or foam cylinder to hold the completed flies. Turning the fly will keep the thick epoxy from sagging and dripping. Some who tie flies make their own, but they are available commercially from most fly shops and catalogs.

HAIR STACKER – These are sometimes called hair eveners, which is perhaps a more descriptive term. These devices are used by stacking hair by the tip end to make it even to make neat wings for dry flies, streamers and the like. Stackers come in several different styles, but most include a flared open tube that fits into a capped butt section. In use, add the hairs tip end down into the stacker, pound the stacker on the bench, then hold the stacker sideways to pull out the open tube with the hairs made even. Stackers come in several different diameters, so choose one that will fit your specific needs.

HAIR PACKERS – Hair packers are designed to pack hair when making hair-bodied flies. Prime examples would be deer-hair bugs for warmwater fishing, but they are used for making the hair bodies of Irresistibles, salmon fly Bombers, and similar hair-bodied patterns. These vary in style, with all having the purpose of pushing the wrapped hair towards the back of the hook shank to get maximum density to the body.

MATERIAL CLIPS – Material clips sometimes come with fly vises, but are available separately. They consist of a small spring collar that fits around the vise sleeve to hold long materials or yet-to-be-wrapped materials out of the way of the tying operation. A variation of this is the stand-up spring that comes with the Regal vise.

MATERIAL DISPENSERS – Material dispensers come in two different styles. One is a divided plastic box (like a lure or fly box) with holes in the bottom of each compartment through which dubbing can be pulled. This is a vast improvement over the originals in which the holes were in the lid and opening the lid to fill an empty compartment messed up the other compartments.

The second type of dispenser is for spooled materials. For this, the Spirit River All Around dispenser is ideal, since it comes with six spools that fit into a divided, locking-lid box that has a slot for pulling out each of the spooled materials. They also make other dispensers and racks for dubbing, lead eyes or hooks and the like.

WASTE CONTAINERS – Waste containers that clamp onto the fly-tying bench at the vise are designed to catch any waste that falls from the vise. They are handy and keep the floor clean when using a clamp-style vise. They generally aren't needed when using a pedestal-style vise, since the materials there will fall onto the bench where they can be swept up.

FLY-TYING BENCHES, DESKS, LAPTOP ORGANIZERS, CARRYING CASES — Many companies make fly-tying work areas and carrying cases. These range from small wood laptop or bench-mounted units (designed to hold the vise and assorted tools and materials) up through beautiful, traditional roll-top or other style desks and benches that are usually fairly costly. Wood and fabric carrying cases for materials are also available. Of all of these, I only use a specialized tying bag that holds all (well, most) of the fly-tying tools and materials that I need on the road for shows and club meetings. I use the Scientific Anglers, J. W. Outfitters model TOTL Tying Bag, but they have three other models also available. These are also ideal when you might wish to tie up new or replacement patterns in a motel room while on a fishing trip.

OTHER TOOLS – Many other tools are available. Bobbins come in many styles and designs, and the styles of scissors number in the dozens. There are tools for folding hackle for making wet flies, for making dubbing brushes for nymphs, plug cutters for making foam cylinders for trout terrestrial bodies, wing cutters, vision magnifiers, dubbing blenders, bobbin rests, tweezers, etc.

More tools are being developed all the time. There are also some esoteric tools for highly specialized fly-tying procedures. One of these neat new tools is the Root's Original Dubbing Machine, designed for making durable dubbing brushes (strands of dubbing) which can be used to make flies of all sizes and types. The above tools, both the basic and accessory, are commonly used and readily available.

Chapter 2
Fly-Tying Materials

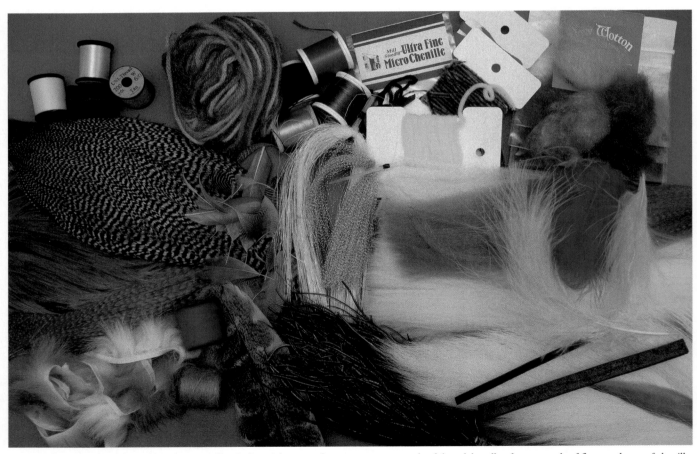

Some of the many materials used in tying trout flies. Left to right, top to bottom: top row; spools of thread, bundle of yarn, spools of floss, packages of chenille and packages of dubbing. Second row; hackle necks, teal and mallard feathers, stranded flash materials, synthetic streamer wing material, and marabou feathers. Third row; feathers, rabbit (Zonker) strips, spools of mohair, turkey feather, peacock herl, bucktail and foam strips,

12   Chapter 2-Fly-Tying Materials

While the tools are necessary to work with the materials, it is the combination of hook, thread, and other materials that are necessary to make the fly into the completed product. Today, there is a vast assortment of materials available, including some of the standard natural materials (such as rooster hackle, bucktail, dubbing fur and peacock herl) along with an assortment of new synthetics in dubbing, stranded materials for wings and body materials. By the time this book is published, undoubtedly there will be more materials that are not even known at the time of this writing.

Some examples and suggestions as to the vast variety of materials available include the following:

HOOKS – Fly-tying hooks are available from great companies such as Mustad, Eagle Claw, Dai-Riki, Daiichi, Tiemco, Gamakatsu, Partridge, VMC and others. For trout, fly hooks typically range in size from about 20 through 10 in even number sizes. Larger (sizes 8, 6, 4, etc.) and smaller (sizes 22, 24, 26, 28) hooks are available for specialty fishing. In addition, trout fly hooks come in fine wire for dry fly fishing on the surface, standard wire for wet flies and heavy wire for nymph and bottom fishing. While the "standard" size of each type and brand of hook varies, most hooks come in a regular length shank for dry fly and wet flies, slightly long for nymphs and even longer for streamer flies. The system for calculating wire size and length is based on an "X" system in which 1X is the equivalent of the next size hook, even through the next size (an odd number) is not made. Thus, a 2X long-shank size 8 hook would have the shank length of a size 6 hook of the same style. A 2X short-shank size 8 hook would be the length of a size 10. A 4X stout size 10 hook would be made of the same wire thickness as a size 6 hook and a 2X fine wire size 14 dry fly hook would have the wire thickness of a size 16. Bends on hooks vary, with the Model Perfect (round bend) best when working with beads, since it has a constant radius that makes it easier to add the right size bead. Most hooks have a straight shank, but there are swimming nymph hooks that have an upward bend to the shank, and scud and shrimp hooks that have a downward curve – both to help simulate the natural creature the fly will imitate. Hooks also have straight, turned up and turned down eyes, with straight and turned down the most common. If you like to tie on your flies with a Turle knot, or any knot in which the leader tippet goes through the eye, you must have a turned up or turned down eye for the leader to be straight with the hook.

Mustad Universal Dry/Wet R50

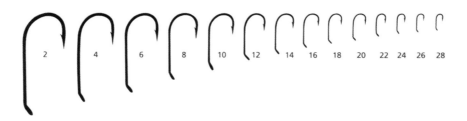

Mustad Streamers R74

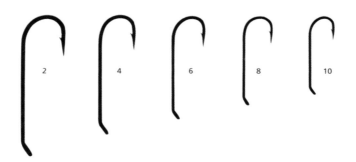

THREAD – There are a number of thread companies making a wide range of thread types in an almost unlimited range of colors and many sizes. As a general rule it is best to use the color thread called for in the pattern, or a color that will complement the fly if you are designing your own. If adding dubbing to make a fly body, or using a material that will become transparent or translucent, use a thread color that will match the body material or one that will contrast with it if you wish a ribbed look.

It is also best to use the finest thread possible for the fly being tied. "Letter" size threads (A, C, D, and E) are used for rod building while the number threads 1/0, 2/0, 3/0 up to 10/0 and rarely 15/0 are common for fly-tying. Most trout flies are tied using size 3/0 for large flies and hair wing/hair body flies, with 6/0 a standard size for most small patterns, and 10/0 used for tiny tricos and midges.

SEALERS – Commonly called head cement as they are applied to the head of the fly, sealers are designed to prevent the thread wrap from unraveling, and to preserve the life of the fly. Many types are available in both petroleum and non-toxic solvent bases. Most are clear, but colors are available.

Standard head cement is usually solvent-based, but companies such as Loon Outdoors make environmentally safe finishes. Many people use nail polish, specifically clear Sally Hansen Hard as Nails finish. It has an easy applicator brush (which can be trimmed and tapered for more precise application), is readily available, dries hard and protects well.

In addition to these sealers, some people are now using epoxy on larger flies. For one who ties trout fly flies, these would be most applicable on large flies such as streamers, bucktails, leeches, and bottom-fished Clousers. Note that with the exception of one epoxy that, at this writing, is not yet on the market, all epoxies will yellow in time. Consider this before tying with them, or tie seasonally so that you are constantly restoring your box with new ties made with new epoxy sealer.

FLOSS – Floss is available in silk or synthetics and is nothing more than a bundle of fine strands of material. It comes in several sizes and many colors and most can be split into smaller strands to make bodies for very small flies. It does require care to work with properly so that the fine strands do

not frizz out. It also requires smooth fingers so as to not catch on rough skin. Some fly-tyers keep a woman's pumice stone available to smooth their fingers before working with such materials.

YARN – Yarn comes in natural or synthetics, with examples being yarns such as natural wool and synthetic Antron or similar fibers. Yarn comes in different diameters and many colors. Many fly-tyers buy their yarn from craft and sewing stores that feature wide varieties and colors of such materials. Yarn by its very nature has a frizzy, fuzzy look, unlike the smooth polished look of a wrapped floss body. Yarn can be tightly wrapped to make a hard body, or untwisted slightly to make a looser wrap with a more buggy look. Specialized yarns include the Glo-Bug yarn that is thick and is available in bright fluorescent colors for tying egg patterns that are used primarily for steelhead and some Pacific salmon fishing. Poly yarn (polypropylene yarn) in clear, white and light colors can be used for bodies, but is primarily used to make wings in spinner and spent-wing patterns of dry flies or trailing shucks in emerger patterns. Leech Yarn and mohair are yarns that have long fuzzy fibers that will make for a very buggy appearance when tying nymphs and some wet flies. Both are very fuzzy yarn-like materials that give a dubbed body look to any fly. Since they both absorb water, they are used primarily for wet flies and nymphs.

CHENILLE – From the French word for caterpillar, chenille is a velvety, tufted material of short strands twisted into a central core and designed as a body material. It is available in many colors and sizes, with or without sparkle fibers added and in a smooth, slightly stiffer grade usually called Ultra Chenille or Vernille. Vernille or Ultra Chenille is used to make the popular San Juan worm. Chenille also comes in speckled colors (tinsel mixed in with the chenille) and two-tone (alternating two colors). All come in many sizes for tying all sizes of flies. Various sizes and colors of sparkly plastic-tinsel "cactus" chenille are also available. Estaz is one popular brand.

DUBBING – Traditionally, dubbing is any material that can be wrapped onto a waxed thread that is then wound around the hook shank to make a fly body. It can be synthetic or natural materials, or a mix of both. It can also be a mix of colors to give it a more lifelike look. Whether natural or synthetic, it is almost always fine, such as the fine underfur from some skins, or fine fur such as opossum, fox, seal, muskrat, buffalo underfur, angora goat, hare's ear or similar natural furs. Some fur has long guard hairs that can be left in or combed out, depending upon the desired buggy or leggy look of the fly body. Some newer synthetic "dubbing" material is designed to be used more as a yarn and wrapped on rather than cut, teased and spun onto waxed thread for wrapping. Examples include Gudebrod E-Z Dub, mohair, or sparkle yarn, a generic term used by Gary LaFontaine for some of the Antron yarns. For small flies, these can usually be separated out into strands to make a slim proportioned body. This makes for far easier and quicker tying than using dubbing, although dubbing is traditional and still best for some dries and for very small flies.

Duck and goose wings are commonly used, taking a matching feather (quill) from each wing and then an identical section from each quill to make the matched (right and left) wings on many wet flies and some dry flies. They can be used natural, or obtained in dyed colors. Dyed colors are necessary for the married wings found on some patterns such as the Parmachene Belle. Turkey is used to make wings similar to duck quill wings along with tent-like wings when tying caddis, stonefly or hopper imitations.

STRANDED FLASH MATERIALS – Stranded flash materials include an ever-increasing range of fibers such as Flashabou, Krystal Flash, Crystal Splash, Tie Well, Flash in a Tube, and others. They are mostly plastic strands, available in a wide range of colors, sometimes in holographic multi-colors, and occasionally twisted for more body, action and flash. They are frequently used for additional flash in wings of streamers, and sometimes sparsely as tails, legs or even body material in nymphs and wet flies.

STRANDED WING MATERIALS – Materials such as Super Hair, Ultra Hair, Aqua Fiber, Unique, Poly Bear, and others are used more for warmwater and saltwater flies, but are also used occasionally in trout streamers. Any of these can be used in place of natural bucktail or other furs for wings in streamers or even in some cases tied sparsely as wings on spent-wing patterns.

TINSELS, WRAPPED FLASH MATERIALS AND WIRE – In the past, only metallic tinsels were available, usually in flat, round and oval, in gold or silver, each in several sizes. Today, the same tinsel is available, along with a much wider range of flat plastic and Mylar "tinsels" available in a wide range of colors. The plastics have both advantages and disadvantages. They will not tarnish as will metallic tinsels, but they are also a little more fragile and more likely to be cut from the fine teeth of a trout. All types of tinsel are used for bodies (Mickey Finn) or ribbing (any of a number of dry flies, wet flies and nymphs).

HACKLE – WET AND DRY – The term hackle refers to the feathers from the neck, cape and throat of a rooster or other fowl. Most often roosters are used for the best dry fly hackle since it has very little webbing (which will absorb water). "Webbing" is the mesh of fine barbules between the fibers that helps to lock the fibers together. Hen hackle is webbier (more and wider web on each hackle feather), softer, soaks up water better and usually the hackle of choice for tying standard wet flies, some soft-hackle wet flies and nymphs. Holding hackle to the light readily shows the amount and location of the webbing. Hen hackle often differs from rooster hackle in coloring and often has a range of speckling that is attractive, but usually unavailable in the rooster hackle.

Hackles are sold loose, but most for trout fishing are used directly from the neck. A neck will have a range of hackle sizes, from small hackles at the upper end (toward the head of the bird) for tying tiny flies to successively larger hackle for larger flies. Saddle hackle is a longer hackle, generally from the back of the bird and is typically used for making streamer wings on trout streamers as well as for hackle on dry and wet flies. Some companies also have necks with very long hackles for winding onto hooks for wet and dry flies.

OTHER FEATHERS – Feathers from partridge, grouse, woodcock, and other game birds (also domesticated guinea hen) are also used for hackle, particularly when tying soft-hackle, sparsely tied wet flies.

Wire is also available in a wide range of diameters and is metallic. Silver, gold, copper, brass and other wires are available along with those with colored finishes. Some are used for most of the body (as with the Brassie nymph), while others are used for fine wire ribbing (as with many dry flies and nymphs). In large sizes they have the advantage of adding weight to nymphs and wet flies.

LEAD WIRE – Lead is available in diameters from about 0.010 to 0.035 inches. It is used to weight streamers and nymphs, usually by wrapping around the body, but sometimes in straight lengths, laid along the hook shank and wrapped in place. More and more companies and individuals are also going to non-lead substitutes, since California, through a restrictive Proposition 65, prohibits lead and a number of other materials in products sold in the state. A body material always covers lead wire, since its only function is to help the fly get deep.

FURS – Rabbit fur is widely used, often available as thin "Zonker strips" for making Zonker flies. It comes in dyed colors for any application. Hare's mask is also used, with fine fibers cut from the ears and mask to make dubbing for certain patterns. The Gold-Ribbed Hare's Ear is one such example. Many other furs can be used in fly-tying, but seem to be less used today than in the past. Mink, mole, mouse, muskrat, possum, bear, beaver, fox, nutria, otter and others are examples. Typically they are used for very specific patterns or for just one part of a fly. Often they are used for dubbing only, or mixed with other furs for a dubbed body. These are in addition to the seal, opossum, Angora goat and buffalo that are used primarily for dubbing material.

HAIR FOR WINGS – Bucktail is typically used for the wings of bucktail style streamers. Bucktail is just what it says – the tail of a deer. It can be used natural, using the brown or white fur from the tail, or it can be dyed, in which the dyed white area only is used. It makes for a nice, streamlined streamer in which one color can be used, or in which stacked colors can be used as with the popular Mickey Finn. Calftail is also a popular wing material for some smaller flies, but less used, since so much of the fur is very kinky. In some cases calftail can be found that is less kinky and is ideal for wings on small flies. In this case, it can be used as a wing on very small streamer flies, as the wing on some hoppers, Trude-style patterns and salmon flies or even as the upright wing on some dry flies. It is generally best on smaller flies, since it does not grow as long as bucktail. Bear is sometimes used when available, although the popular polar bear, favored for the translucency of the fur, is now prohibited for importation or sale.

BODY HAIR – Body hair is a hollow hair from the bodies of deer, elk, antelope, moose and caribou. Deer, antelope and elk are most often used in fly-tying, and less used for trout flies than for warmwater bass flies. However, flies such as the Irresistible and Rat-Faced McDougal do have deer-hair bodies; the hair spun or stacked in place and then trimmed to shape.

BEADS – Beads are a relatively new addition to the fly-tying scene and used both as the head of a fly (metallic weighted beads) or as part of the attraction of the body or tail, as with glass beads. Tungsten beads, heavier than lead, are sold for weighting the head of a nymph or wet fly, and other metallic beads in various painted colors and metallic finishes are available.

Metallic cones in various sizes and colors are also available, and give a pointed, tapered look to a fly while also adding weight to the front end. They are added the same way that metallic beads are added, with the thread and fly tied in place after the cone is slipped onto the hook.

Glass beads are also used on the head of a fly when less weight is desired, as well as threaded onto the hook shank or laced into the body or tail of various scud, shrimp, trailing shuck, emerger and other patterns of nymphs.

LEAD, NON-LEAD, PRISM AND OTHER EYES – While the term dumbbell and hourglass are sometimes used interchangeably, there are differences. The dumbbell eyes are shaped like a miniature dumbbell and thus sometimes difficult to center exactly on a hook shank. The hourglass eyes, shaped like the namesake, self-center on the hook. They are available in lead, lead substitute, chrome, brass and other finishes as well as painted and with painted pupils.

In addition, many other eyes for flies are available. Prism eyes can be placed on the head of any streamer fly (they must be coated with head cement or epoxy to stay on), small ball-monofilament eyes for nymphs are available, as well as bead-chain eyes as a substitute for lead hourglass eyes on streamers and Clousers.

BRAIDED BODY MATERIALS – Braided body materials include Kreinick, Bodi Braid and other rope-like materials that are woven into a braided body wrap. Basically designed for the clothing trades, some of these have made their way into the fly-tying mainstream and are ideal for bodies on simple wet flies and streamers. Many colors are available

MARABOU, CHICKABOU – Marabou, originally from the African marabou stork and now available from turkey feathers, is very soft and has a lot of action in the water. If used in the wing of a fly, it mats down, but on a pause, will fluff out or blossom to attract trout. It is used in simple streamers and also in dark colors as the tail of woolly buggers. A similar more recent material is Chickabou, soft chicken hen fibers that have action in the water similar to that of marabou.

PEACOCK HERL, OSTRICH AND EMU – Trout seem to like flies made with peacock herl. Lots of patterns include this material that is sparkly and also has a buggy iridescence to it. It is usually wound on as a body, but sometimes used as a topping on streamer flies. Similar materials with a larger, fluffier herl are ostrich and emu, although they are far less used in tying flies than the buggy-looking peacock.

SYNTHETIC CUT WINGS – Fly-tyers have long tried to make synthetic wings for dry flies, dragonflies, caddis, etc. Examples have been veined but poor materials of the past, and the use of the poly wing material is one more attempt in this direction, although it is very suggestive rather than highly imitative. Aire Flow wings are a modern example of these that work well. The material is translucent, veined like the natural wings, buoyant and available in a half-dozen colors for different flies, from Dark Hendricksons to Light Cahills. Three sizes are available to match mayflies from 12 through 22 and caddis from 6 through 16. They are available in brown and olive hopper wings also.

VINYL/PLASTIC BODY MATERIAL AND RIBBING – Just as there have been attempts to develop synthetic wings, there have also been attempts to find a synthetic translucent insect-like body material. The first successful venture in this was Larva Lace, although some other similar materials are also available. Larva Lace is very thin, colored translucent tubing that can be stretched and wrapped around a hook shank to make a life-like segmented body. A similar flat (really half round) material also works well as a tough plastic ribbing on flies. Some tyers use thin strips of latex for the same purpose when tying nymphs.

RUBBER/SILICONE LEGS – Flexible, synthetic legs are used more when tying bass and panfish flies, but they also have their place in trout flies. They are most commonly used when tying flies such as the Madame X and Bitch Creek nymph, or as additional attraction when tying terrestrials such as hoppers, crickets, beetles, etc. Legs are available in rubber, silicone, Spandex and other materials, in solid colors as well as barred or mottled designs.

BODY TUBING – Body tubing consists of braided plastic tubular materials such as Corsair and E-Z Body. The tubing comes in many diameters and several colors. It is ideal for making simple and easy baitfish-like bodies for streamer flies by slipping it in place and tying off at body ends.

MYLAR TUBING – Mylar tubing is shiny, thin-walled, braided tubing that is also used for making streamer bodies. It is available in several sizes and commonly comes in gold or silver, and sometimes other metallic-like finishes. It is sold with a cord core which must be pulled out before using the tubing. The most common use for this is when tying bodies for Zonkers and Matukas.

FOAM – Both closed-cell and open-cell foam is used in tying trout flies. The open-cell foam will absorb water and is commonly used as a body or underbody on some nymph patterns. It is available in a lot of colors and several thicknesses in strip and sheet form. Closed-cell foam will not absorb water and is ideal for making a wide range of parachute posts, terrestrials, and sometimes pods to help float emergers. It is available in a wide range of colors and in cylinders in several diameters. It is also available in shaped bodies (ants, etc.) as well as strips and sheets in several different thicknesses.

Chapter 3

Fly-Tying Methods

Note: In these tying directions, the assumption is that the fly-tyer is right-handed and thus will have the jaws of the fly-tying vise facing to the right. Thus, where right or left hands are mentioned, it is based on this premise. Also note that these methods of working are not the only methods of accomplishing the many tying methods used with fly-tying. They are one or two proven methods that work well and which allow creation of good-looking, effective flies. For encyclopedic information on the many ways of working with fly-tying materials and accomplishing fly-tying tasks, check out the 444-page book, THE FLY TIER'S BENCHSIDE REFERENCE TO TECHNIQUES AND DRESSING STYLES, by Ted Leeson and Jim Schollmeyer.

ORDER OF TYING – Many beginning tiers don't think of an order of tying – they just start by tying the thread onto the hook at some point. This is a mistake, since where and how you start, and in which order you place the materials, can make a big difference in the appearance of the completed fly and the ease by which it is completed. The recipes for each of our one hundred top patterns will contain a suggested order of tying materials, but some general suggestions are as follows:

Dry flies – Dry flies are often best started by starting the thread about 1/3rd the shank length in back of the hook eye, then tying on the wings, tip forward and then raising them to an upright position. Note that this method is generally used for wings whether upright, upright and divided, fan wing or spent. It also generally applied whether the wings are hackle tips, hackle fibers, fur, synthetic cut wings or synthetic fibers. After positioning the wings, wrap the thread to the bend to add the tails. Tie on the ribbing and then the body material or make the dubbing on the tying thread. Wrap the thread forward and wrap the body and any ribbing up to the previously tied-on upright wings. Then tie in the hackle and wind in front and back of the wings. Before tying off, wrap the thread through the hackle for added strength, then complete the head, tie off and whip finish. Parachute dry flies are basically tied the same way. Add the post or wings before progressing to the tail, then add the body, and finally the hackle that is wound horizontally around the post or wings.

Wet flies – Begin your wet fly by tying on at about the middle of the hook shank, then wrap the thread to just forward of the bend. Tie in any tail material, then tie in the ribbing/body material, wrap the thread forward, follow with the wrapped body and any ribbing, then tie them off. Tie in a hackle, wind it to make collar-style, then tie in paired wings clipped from duck quills. Trim the excess and tie off at the head. An alternative to the full hackle is to tie in hackle or other throat fibers underneath the fly at the head and then finish as above.

Nymphs - Tie in at mid-shank, then wrap to the bend to tie in any tails. Tie in any ribbing and body material, then wrap the thread 2/3rds up the hook shank. Then wrap up the body, followed by the ribbing. Tie off, then tie in a section of quill (often turkey quill), followed by the stem of a short length of a game feather. Add more body material and wrap it forward to just in back of the hook eye. Wind the game feather forward and tie it down. At this point, the tips can be pulled under to make a beard hackle, or pulled to the side to make legs or a semblance of gills. Follow by folding over the quill to make the wing casing. Trim and tie off to complete the fly. This is just one example of a nymph, since others may include a bead head, or a simple tie of tail, body material, legs and wrapped head. Note that nymphs vary widely in patterns, designs, and tying styles.

Terrestrials – Terrestrials such as beetles, ants, hoppers and crickets are tied in a number of ways. Most terrestrials can be started by tying on in the middle of the hook shank. Following this, wrap back or forward to build up the body or to add the foam, deer hair or other body materials used to make ants or beetles. For crickets and hoppers, tie on in back of the hook eye, then add the deer hair or foam for the body, then any turkey quill for wings and any hackle to finish the fly. Some terrestrials, such as the McMurray ant, are tied completely in the middle to hold the previously prepared balsa or foam abdomen and thorax and the wound hackle.

Streamers and bucktails — To make a simple streamer without a tail, tie the thread on at the head, add the tinsel of body material and then wrap the material down to the hook bend and back up again to tie off at the head. A body and ribbing can be handled the same way, or begun at the tail of the fly and wrapped forward. Add the wing or wing components, including any topping, followed by the throat. The wing may be two sets of saddle hackles (streamer) or a bucktail wing (single or stacked bucktail colors). After trimming, the head is completed and the fly tied off. A variation of this for streamers with a tail is to tie in at mid-shank, wrap thread to the rear to tie in the tail, then wrap forward to tie in the body, which is wrapped fore and aft to cover the hook shank. The remainder of the fly with wing, topping and throat is completed as above.

TYING THE THREAD ONTO THE HOOK – Thread can be tied onto the hook at any point, but always involves the same method. For best results, hold the tag end of the thread in the left hand below the hook and the bobbin in the right hand above the hook. Make a few turns of the thread (right hand) around the hook shank so that the wraps are parallel. Then make a few additional wraps around the hook shank in which the thread crosses over the previous wraps. It is this wrapping method, and the constant tension on the thread, that maintains the tight wrap. An alternative to this is to add a little head cement to the hook shank before tying down to prevent the thread and subsequent body materials from slipping or rotating on the hook.

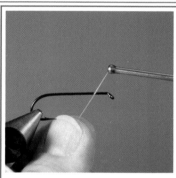

Step 1 - To tie the thread onto the hook, first hold the tag end and the bobbin (if used) over the top of the hook shank as shown.

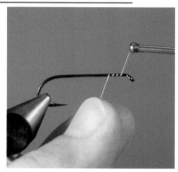

Step 2 - Then wrap the standing end of the thread (bobbin) around the hook shank two or more times. Gaps are shown here for clarity – normally the thread wraps would be tight.

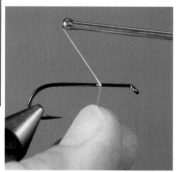

Step 3 - To lock the thread in place, wrap or wind over (cross over) the previous wraps as shown here.

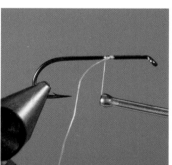

Step 4 - Pull the thread down and make several more winds of the thread to securely lock the thread in place.

Step 5 - Close-up of the initial thread wrapping shown with heavy cord and a large hook.

Step 6 - Close-up as above – here the thread has been crossed over the previous wraps to lock the thread and wrap in place. Shown with heavy cord and oversize hook.

USING THREAD AS RIBBING – If using thread as ribbing on a fly, make the tag end of the tie-down process longer than normal (several inches at least) and do not clip it. In most cases, then tie in the tail or tag followed by the body material or adding dubbing to the working thread. Then, after the body is wrapped in place, use this tag end for the ribbing to spiral wrap up the shank and over the body. Tie off this tag end with the working thread. In some cases, you may want to reverse the ribbing wrap (counter wrap) to help secure and protect the body material. Naturally, this technique of using thread for ribbing (regular wrap or counter wrap) only works if the desired ribbing thread color is the same as the working thread. This same method can be used to tie on in the middle or forward third of the hook shank to leave a tag end to secure folded over deer hair when making bullet head flies such as the Thunder Creek series.

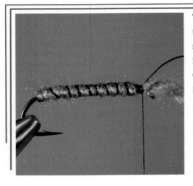

To use thread as ribbing leave a long tag end at the end of the hook shank, tie down the body and wind forward and then wind the thread over the wrapped body to make a ribbing as shown here.

...you may want to reverse the ribbing wrap (counter wrap) to help secure and protect the body material.

TYING TAILS – Tails are tied on dry flies, some wet flies, some streamers, and many nymphs. Since the tail is usually the thinnest part of the fly, you want minimal bulk here. The way to achieve this is to begin the thread wrap on the hook shank farther forward (where the body will cover it) and then wrap the thread to the tail area before adding the tail fibers. For best results, use the full length of tail material to cover the hook shank even if tying down only a short tail. Use the soft-loop method outlined below for this. Hold the tail fibers in place over the hook shank with the left hand. Bring the thread straight up with the right hand, pinch with the left index finger and thumb, then straight down on the far side of the hook before pulling tight. Repeat several times. This keeps the tail straight and on top of the hook shank, rather than cocked to one side. Note that, in some cases, it may be advantageous to add the body material and ribbing to the hook shank before adding the tail to get a smooth transition from the tail to the body and up the hook shank. For the same reason, do not clip the tail materials immediately forward of the tail tie-down point. Instead, clip them so that they will extend forward and will be covered by the body. This will prevent any lumpiness in the tail and make for a smooth tapered body.

To tie tails in place, leave enough of the tail forward of the hook so that any subsequent body material will have a level base for tying. Failure to do this can result in a "stepped" appearance, particularly when using tinsel, stripped quill or stripped peacock.

...it may be advantageous to add the body material and ribbing to the hook shank before adding the tail to get a smooth transition...

MAKING THE SOFT LOOP TO TIE MATERIALS IN PROPER POSITION – What fly-tyers typically call a soft loop is a method by which any material can be positioned properly on the hook. Typically, it is used to position tails, streamer wings, throat hackle, dry fly wings, or when stacking deer hair. It allows placing a material precisely so that it will not slip to the side or become cocked or angled. To do this, hold the material (let's say a streamer wing) in place on top of the hook shank with the left hand. Bring the thread straight up with the right hand, pinch it with the left hand, then bring it straight down on the far side of the hook before pulling tight. An easy way to do this is to rock your left index finger and thumb back and forth to open and close their grip to hold the wing or other material, while pinching the thread in the pull upward and then downward. Repeat several times. This keeps the wing straight and on top of the hook shank, rather than cocked to one side. This method is important to master – and it is easy to master – to secure all types of materials. Even though less important with ribbing and body material, it still helps to minimize the number of necessary wraps and to make sure that the material is located where you want it to be for the best looking fly.

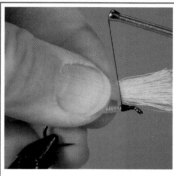

Step 1 - Making the soft loop to properly position materials begins by holding the material (in this case, bucktail) and then bringing the thread straight up alongside the material.

Step 2 - Roll the fingers forward to grasp the thread as shown here.

Step 3 - Then bring the loose thread down on the far side of the hook shank and material being tied down.

Step 4 - Make one or two soft wraps like this, and then pull the thread tight to secure the material as bucktail is being secured here. Note that the bucktail is on top of the hook – not skewed to one side.

Step 5 - A top view of the above shows that the material (bucktail) is in alignment with the hook and properly positioned.

Step 6 - A top view of bucktail tied in place without using the soft loop shows that the material is pulled to one side and skewed out of line.

Step 7 - A side view of the bucktail tied in place without the soft loop wrap shows the material pulled to one side of the hook.

...rock your left index finger and thumb back and forth to open and close their grip...

TYING DRY FLY WINGS – Dry fly wings are tied straight up, even if later they are splayed to the side (divided wing) or placed horizontally (spent-wing). The exception is found in most caddis and stonefly patterns that have wings angled on top of the body or sharply angled to the rear. For dry flies (mayfly imitations), begin by placing the tips of the wing forward and tie the butt ends down, tying to a spot about 1/3rd the length of the shank back from the hook eye as the fulcrum point. Wrap in front of the wings and around the base to force them into an upright position. The same method can be employed if the wings are hackle points or fan wings. In some cases, it helps to wrap in front of just a part of the wing bundle (particularly when using calf or deer hair), followed by wrapping in front of additional parts of the bundle. This helps to raise and hold the wing upright. By tying them in with the base facing to the rear, it is easier to hide the base with the built-up body that will cover this, and also allows for the tapering effect of the body.

To tie in dry fly wings, first clip and position the wings for proper length for the hook and then tie in with the tips forward as shown.

Raise the dry fly wings up by pulling them into an upright position and then winding thread in front of the wing to hold the wing in an upright, vertical position.

TYING DIVIDED WINGS – Tie divided dry fly wings when the wings are of hackle fibers just as you do an upright wing, with the following additional steps. Once the wing has been bound down to the hook shank and raised up to a vertical position, use a bodkin to divide the wing into two parts – right and left. (This is not necessary if the wings are quill section wings, since the division between the two wings will be obvious.) Once the two halves of the hackle fiber wings are divided, use the tying thread to crisscross and figure-8 wrap through the two wings bundles to separate them into two equal and properly angled wings, each one approximately 30 degrees from vertical. It also helps to make one or two turns around the base of each wing to separate it from the other and from the rest of the tying procedure. If tying divided wings that are of quill sections or cut wings from a hackle, the separation of the two wings will be obvious. However, the figure-8 wraps with the thread are still necessary to angle the wings slightly to the side.

Step 1 - To tie divided wings, use a bodkin to separate the upright wing into two equal bundles.

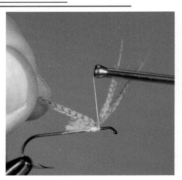

Step 2 - To secure the divided wing, after the wing has been tied upright and separated, use the thread to wind between the two bundles to secure them into the divided position.

Step 3 - Front view of the divided wing

...make one or two turns around the base of each wing to separate it from the others...

TYING TRAILING SHUCKS – Trailing shucks are a relatively recent development in fly-tying, and consist of nothing more than a tail of a material that will simulate the casting of a nymph as it shucks it on the surface when transforming into the adult or dun stage. As such, they are tied on in place of a tail. They usually consist of a whitish or light colored yarn or similar material, often the length of a standard tail. Sparkle Duns, developed by Craig Mathews, are basically Comparaduns with a trailing shuck of Z-lon or Antron in place of a standard tail.

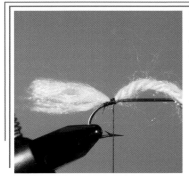

Here a trailing shuck is tied in place using a short length of yarn that has been frayed out to make it like a trailing shuck of a nymph/dun. Other materials can also be used.

...they are tied on in place of a tail. They usually consist of a whitish or light colored yarn...

TYING SPENT WINGS – Spent wings are wings that are laying flat – that is, horizontal to the surface as would a spinner mayfly after being exhausted from mating. Spent-wing mayflies are those that are dead or dying on the surface of the water. Spent wings, just as with upright or divided wings, can be made of many materials including cut wings, hackle, hackle tips, calf tail, and stiff fiber synthetics. While there are many methods of tying spent wings, most involve first tying on the material just as you would a divided or upright wing. For this, tie in the material tips forward with the tie-down point about 1/3rd of the shank length in back of the eye. Then separate the bundle into two, pulling the far side bundle back and then figure-8 wrapping thread between the two bundles. Continue by pulling the near side bundle back and repeat the same so that you are tying the thread in a figure-8 around each individual bundle. In doing this, make sure that the bundles are flat or horizontal and at right angles to the plane of the hook. An alternative method for synthetic fiber wings (poly, poly yarn, sparkle yarn, etc.) is to make the bundle approximately the length of the two wings together, then position it at an angle on top of the hook shank, tie down with a few turns of thread and then alternate the tie to make an "X" of wraps on top of the wing. This will help stabilize the wing while also making sure that it stays in a spent position and at right angles to the hook shank.

Step 1 - To tie spent wings, begin as you do any wing, by tying them in tips forward as shown.

Step 2 - Separate the wings into two bundles and then pull each bundle back and horizontal, then hold it in position with tying thread as shown.

Step 3 - Top view of spent wings.

...make sure that the bundles are flat or horizontal and at right angles to the plane of the hook.

MAKING THE DIVIDED OR FORKED TAIL – There are several ways to divide or fork a tail for certain dry flies. One way is to build up a small lump of thread immediately in back of where you will attach the tail. The fibers are then forced to the sides and will not align with the axis of the hook shank. The same thing can be done with a very small wrap of dubbing, if making a dubbing body. It is also possible to tie in the tail, then use alternate wraps around the hook shank and each of the tails (right and left) to force the tails to splay out to the sides.

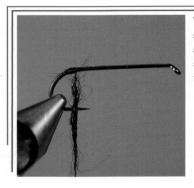

To make a divided tail, first tie in a small bit of dubbing to make for a small lump at the end of the hook shank to divide the fibers when the tail is tied down.

Here the tail fibers have been tied down and split by the small bump of dubbing previously tied in place.

TYING SYNTHETIC CUT WINGS – Synthetic cut wings, like those from Aire-Flow, have both dry fly wings joined together, almost like butterfly wings without the body. To tie them in place, fold the center point around the hook shank from underneath, then crisscross the thread in front of and in back of the wings to hold this before making figure-8 wraps around the separate wings to place them in a divided wing position. Tie spent-wing patterns with the wings on top of the hook shank, then wrap around the center stem alternatively from front to back and back to front. Tie down caddis and hopper wings by folding the wing over the top of the hook shank and any underlying materials and then using the soft loop to pull the thread down and the wing into proper position.

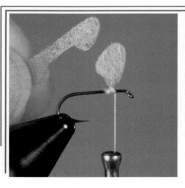

To tie in cut wings such as the synthetic wings from Aire Flow, fold the wings around the hook shank (both wings are attached at the center) and then wrap thread around and on each side of the wing as shown to secure them in an upright position. Cut wings are also shown here.

Angled view of synthetic cut wings tied in place.

TYING BODIES – After tying in any tail materials, begin a body by tying down the ribbing first (if applicable) then the body material, using a tag end of the body material as long as the hook shank. Then wrap the thread forward to the tie-off point, wrapping over the tag end of the body material. Wrap the body material around the hook shank to the tie-down point, and secure with two or more wraps of thread. Then follow with a spiral wrap of the ribbing to the tie-down point and secure the ribbing. An alternative method with some body materials and some dubbing is to start at the midpoint of the hook shank to build up more bulk there before wrapping to the tail and then back up to tie off with the thread. This will give more of a natural tapered appearance to the body. With the ribbing tied down by the body material at the rear of the fly, wrap it forward and tie off where the body ends.

Step 1 - To tie in a body, several techniques can be used. For this, the tail has been tied down first and the body material (yarn) tied in preparatory to wrapping forward after winding the thread forward.

Step 2 - Here the body material is being wound forward after being tied down. The thread was wrapped forward prior to this, and after the yarn was tied in place.

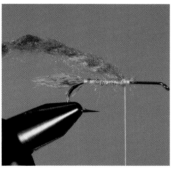

Step 3 - An alternate Method for tying bodies of chenille, yarn and floss is to tie them down in at mid-shank, as shown here.

Step 4 - Once tied down at mid-shank, then wrap forward, back to the tail and then back to the tie-off point where the wings and hackle will be tied down. This makes for two layers of wrap at the rear of the fly and three layers of wrap at the forward end of the fly.

TYING RIBBING – Ribbing is a spaced wrap of tinsel, wire, thread, or other material that adds flash or color to a body and/or simulates the segmented body of the fly. One way to do this is to tie down the tag end of the ribbing immediately after tying the tail in place, assuming a tail is added to the fly. Then tie the tag end of the body material down. This allows wrapping the body material forward (after wrapping the tying thread forward first) so that the ribbing follows naturally over and around the body from the first wrap. If working with metal tinsels, it also helps to cut the tag end of the tinsel on a sharp taper so that the tied-down tinsel does not make a sharp lump under the fly body. It also makes it easier to begin the ribbing wrap around the body. In some cases, the ribbing may fall into the spacing between the body material wrap. This can happen with chenille and some yarns. If you don't want this, an alternative is to wrap the ribbing in the opposite direction (counterwrap) so that the wrap is angled, rather than parallel to the body wrap. Thus, rather than wrapping up and over the body on the front side of the fly, the wrap would be up and over on the far side of the fly until tying off in back of the head. An alternative method of adding ribbing is to tie it in with the body material at the middle of the hook shank, then wrap the body over the ribbing to the rear of the fly before tapering and completing the body. Then spiral the ribbing forward over the body and tie off.

Step 1 - To tie in ribbing, first tie in the tail (if used – none is shown here) then the ribbing material (a fine braid is used here) and then the body material.

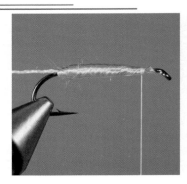

Step 2 - Continue by winding the thread forward, followed by the body material, which is then tied off as shown here. The ribbing extends to the rear, held in place with a materials clip.

Step 3 - Spiral wrap the ribbing material over the body as shown here, and then tie off at the front with the tying thread.

In some cases, the ribbing may fall into the spacing between the body material wrap.

TYING DRY FLY HACKLE – After tying in the wings, tail and body, add the dry fly hackle. To do this, splay out the fibers of the hackle and then tie in the butt end immediately in back of the wings. Trim any excess butt end. Use hackle pliers to wind the hackle around the hook shank, alternating wraps in front of and in back of the wings. With enough hackle wound in place, tie off with several wraps of tying thread, clip the excess, finish the head and tie off with a whip finish. If you wish to reinforce the hackle, weave several turns of thread through the hackle before making the head and tying off.

Step 1 - To tie in a dry fly hackle, prepare the hackle and strip the last 1/4 inch to better secure it with the tying thread as shown here. Note that hackle is usually tied in last, but for photo clarity, no other materials are shown here.

Step 2 - Using hackle pliers, wind the hackle around the hook shank as shown and then complete, tie off the hackle with the tying thread.

Step 3 - Finish the dry fly hackle by using fine tip scissors to clip out only the end of the hackle not being used, then wind thread through the hackle to reinforce it.

...wind the hackle around the hook shank, alternating wraps in front of and in back of the wings...

TYING DRY FLY PARACHUTE POSTS OR WINGS – Since parachute hackle is wound parallel to the hook shank instead of at right angles to it, and thus can not be wound around the hook shank, it must have a base upon which it can be tied and wrapped. Usually this base is the upright wings added to the fly, although for spent-wing or no-wing patterns, a small post of foam, hair or other material can be used. These wings or posts are tied in exactly the same way as are upright wings on any dry fly. If posts are used, often they are kept long initially, and held vertical for support with a suspension arm or gallows tool. The gallows tool is nothing more than a spring arm to hold the post upright while winding the hackle. This aids in winding the hackle around the post or wing, after which the post can be cut short.

To tie in a post or wing for a parachute hackle, proceed as you did for tying in dry fly wings. Posts or wings can be used and in this case a wing of calf fur is being used.

Wrap in front of the wing or post as shown and then wrap around the post/wing to firm and rigid the base.

TYING DRY FLY PARACHUTE HACKLE – Parachute hackle is tied exactly as is regular hackle, except that it is wound around the base of the wings or a parachute post in place of being wound around the hook shank. Tie in the butt of the hackle at the base of the wings (or post) and use hackle pliers to hold the hackle tip while winding it horizontally around the wings or post. Tie off with the tying thread, trim the excess hackle and complete the head on the fly. (Note – you will have to trim the forward part of the hackle or hold it up out of the way while finishing the head and tying off with a whip finish.)

Step 1 - To tie in dry fly parachute hackle, tie in along the hook shank and next to the wing/post as shown.

Step 2 - To wrap the hackle, use the hackle pliers carefully and with light tension to wind the hackle around the base stem of the wing/post as shown.

Step 3 - Continue to wrap until you have sufficient hackle to support the fly, then tie off with the thread.

Step 4 - Completed parachute dry fly hackle, top view.

TYING WET FLY WINGS – Wet fly wings are usually tied on after the throat or collar hackle is added to the fly. Basically, the wings are the last material added before the fly is finished. Wet fly wings are tied facing to the rear, the position they will have in the completed fly. Most often, wet fly wings are quill sections, but these can be tied in four different ways. Since the quill sections have a point to them, and since they have a curvature to each section, the wings can be tied point up or point down, and with the concave side of the quill flared out or facing each other. Most wet flies are tied with the wing tips or points down so that the wing has a smooth curve to it, rather than a peaked pointed look. Also, most are tied with the concave side flared out, to give the wing more body and lifelike appearance. Wings from hackle fibers are also possible. These are tied as a bundle placed on top of the fly and tied down to give the fly a winged appearance. Hackle fiber wings like this are not as noticeable as are quill wings, and give more of a nymph-like appearance to the fly. In tying down all of these wing styles, use the soft loop to secure and position the wing directly on top of the hook shank.

To tie in wet fly wings, prepare the hackle fibers or as in this case, the paired quill wing sections. Hold them in position on top of the hook and make a soft loop with the tying thread to pull the wings down and secure them. These wings are shown without hackle, which often accompanies wet flies.

Most often, wet fly wings are quill sections, but these can be tied in four different ways.

TYING WET FLY COLLAR HACKLE - There are several ways to tie in a wet fly collar hackle, which is wound completely around the hook shank. One is to tie in the hackle in front of the body and then use hackle pliers to wind the hackle several times around the hook shank at the same point. Tie off with the working thread, and clip the excess hackle. Use the fingers of your left hand to fold and flare back the hackle, then wrap around the forward part of this with the thread to keep the hackle flared towards the rear. A second way is to fold the hackle over itself along the center quill. You can do this by hand, or tools are made for this purpose. Then tie down the butt end of the folded hackle. With the hackle fibers facing to the rear, use hackle pliers to wind the hackle around the hook shank, then tie off and finish as above to keep the hackle flared back. With most wet flies, wings are added on top of the hackle after this step.

Step 1 - To tie in a wet fly collar hackle, tie in as you did with the dry fly hackle. Usually this is tied in after all other materials have been added with the exception of the wings, which are added last.

Step 2 - Wind the hackle around the hook shank as shown, as you would do with a dry fly hackle.

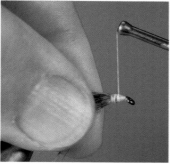

Step 3 - Use your thumb and fore finger to pull back the hackle and hold it in place while winding thread in front of the hackle to help flare it into a rear-angled position.

Step 4 - If wings are not added (some wet flies lack them) you can finish the fly with a whip finish as shown here. The whip finish has been made and the bodkin is pulling the loop up to secure the knot.

TYING OFF – HALF HITCHES – Half hitches are just what they sound like and just what they look like in any knot book. They are a loop taken around the head of the fly with the loop capturing one strand of the standing thread. To do this, maintain tension and loop the thread around the half hitch tool, then place the half hitch tool on the eye of the hook, and slide the loop off of the tapered end of the half hitch tool and onto the fly head. They are also possible to do without a half hitch tool by maintaining tension on the thread wrapped around the hook, folding a loop in the thread and positioning it on the head of the fly. This method also makes it possible to add a half hitch anywhere on the fly as an added lock or security to the tying process after each material is added. It is also possible to add several half hitches – one after the other – for additional locking. A final alternative is to make several loops with the thread around the half hitch tool before pulling it all tight. If doing this, the basic result is the same as a whip finish, although it may not pull up quite as nicely.

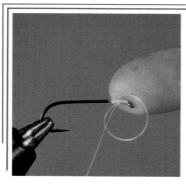

To make a half hitch fold the thread over as for the whip finish, but do not wrap it around the hook shank. Instead, position the loop over the hook shank as shown and pull the thread to secure this locking knot.

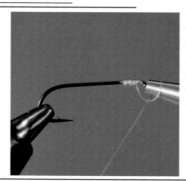

It is also possible to make a half hitch in the end of a fly using a half hitch tool. These are shaped like the end of a pencil but with a hole in the end to fit over the hook eye. The come in various sizes to fit all hook eye sizes.

TYING WET FLY THROAT HACKLE – A throat hackle is a small bundle of hackle tied in at the throat directly under the fly. It can be hackle or bits of fur such as calf tail, bucktail, rabbit, synthetics or other materials. Length varies with the pattern, but it is generally shorter than the hook shank or at least does not extend beyond the hook point. There are two ways to tie in such a throat since it is not wound around the hook shank as with a traditional collar hackle. One way is to keep the hook in the basic tying position and add the throat. To do this, pull the working thread down, and hold the throat material under the fly. Use the fingers of your left hand to pinch the thread, then pull up straight on the thread to capture the throat with the thread loop. This step, identical to the soft-loop method used on top of a fly hook to mount a streamer wing, is necessary to keep the throat straight and in

line with the hook shank. Make a second identical wrap and then several final wraps. Trim the material in front of the thread wraps, and then complete the head of the fly, since adding a throat is often the last step in tying. A second method of adding a throat is to remove the hook from the vise and remount it hook point up. (A variation to this, if you have a true rotary vise, is to rotate the vise 180 degrees to position the hook point up.) Then, with the hook point up and the shank horizontal, pull up the thread, position throat material and then pull down on the thread on the backside of the hook shank to capture the throat material. The technique is the same as the previous one, only the position of the fly is reversed to make it easier to hold the throat in position and add it to the fly.

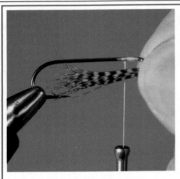

Step 1 - To tie in a wet fly throat hackle, hold the hackle fibers in place under the hook shank as shown.

Step 2 - Make a soft loop but in this case make it down and then up to secure the throat hackle directly under the body and in line with the hook shank.

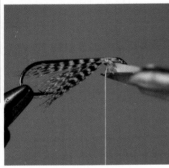

Step 3 - Use fine-tip scissors to clip any forward excess fibers from the throat hackle as shown here.

Step 4 - An alternative method to make a throat hackle which is often easier is to turn the fly over in the vise so that the point is up and then position the throat hackle and make a standard up/down soft loop to hold the hackle in place.

TYING BUTTS – Butts are tied in some wet flies and a few dry flies to simulate an egg sac or just for added color on attractor patterns. To add a butt, tie in butt material after tying down the tail of the fly, then wrap the thread forward a

few turns. Make one or more turns of the butt material around the hook shank and tie off with the tying thread. Then tie in the body and ribbing (if used) for the rest of the fly.

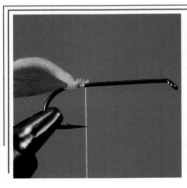

To tie in a butt, do so after the tail has been tied in place as shown here. Here chenille is being use, but several butt materials are possible.

Once the butt is tied in place, wind the thread forward a short distance and make a very few wraps with the butt material before tying off as shown here. Then the rest of the body is tied down and then wrapped forward.

TYING OFF – WHIP FINISH – The technique of tying off with a whip finish is no different than the method used to make a whip finish on the end of a rope learned by Boy Scouts and Girl Scouts. To make a whip finish, make a large loop, then lay the working thread parallel to the hook shank. Use the loop to make wraps around the head and the working thread. After four or more turns, pull the working thread to pull the loop tight against the head and complete the whip finish. A tip here is to use a bodkin to hold the loop and keep the thread from twisting. Twisting may make it impossible to pull all of the thread under the whip finish wraps.

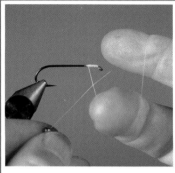

Step 1 - To tie off with a whip finish, make a large loop and then fold it over with your fingers as shown.

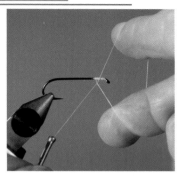

Step 2 - Continue to make the whip finish as above, and rotate your hand to place the pads of your fingers away from you so that one finger can rotate the loop of thread around the hook shank.

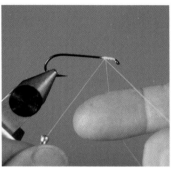

Step 3 - Bring the thread up and over the hook shank and then back to the original position of the thread loop as shown.

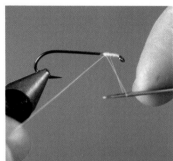

Step 4 - Make a number of these wraps (four to six) and then use a bodkin to hold the loop and pull it up tightly to the head of the fly. Using the bodkin prevents the thread from twisting and tangling.

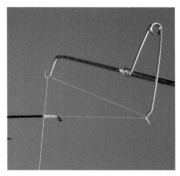

Step 5 - It is also possible to use a whip finish tool to make the whip finish. Several styles are available, but all come with instructions as to their proper use. They work well.

...use a bodkin to hold the loop and keep the thread from twisting.

SEALING THE HEAD – EPOXY – Larger heads on streamer flies can be coated with epoxy. This is not recommended for small flies, since epoxy is too thick and may cover the hook eye, or mat hackle on even large wets and dries. Any good clear epoxy will work, but note that most epoxies will color to amber in time. To use epoxy, first measure and mix the proper amounts of epoxy and hardener on a small mixing surface. Mix thoroughly, or until you can no longer see the swirls of the two different liquids in the mixed batch. Use a bodkin and carefully add the epoxy to all parts of the head, making sure that you cover the head completely, without touching the hook eye or getting epoxy in the materials. Once coated, place the fly in a slow rpm fly rotator that will rotate the fly until the epoxy cures. This will prevent sagging and will make for a smooth finish to the fly head. Most fly-tyers use five-minute epoxy. The advantage of using epoxy on flies where it is possible is that only one coat is necessary.

SEALING THE HEAD – HEAD CEMENT – To keep the fly head and whip finish from unraveling, a coating of cement is a must. Many cements – often called head cements for the obvious reason that it is used on the head of the fly – are available. Since the heads of most trout flies are small, the best application is with a bodkin, applying a small drop to the head and using the bodkin to make sure that the liquid cement is distributed evenly over the fly head without touching the rest of the fly or the hackle. Larger heads on streamer flies can be coated with a small brush, such as is available with nail polish bottles. Many anglers use clear nail polish for coating fly heads, with Sally Hansen Hard As Nails a favorite. Note that with any cement, multiple coats are necessary to properly protect the fly head. A tip here when using any brush applicator is to use scissors to trim and taper the brush for more precise application.

To seal the head, use head cement or fingernail polish. Dip into the head cement with a bodkin as shown and apply carefully to the wrapped head of the fly.

...with any cement, multiple coats are necessary to properly protect the fly head.

STACKING (EVENING) HAIR BUNDLES – Most natural fur used for wings, hair bodies, tails and streamer wings requires removal of the underfur before use as well as evening the tip ends to make for a better appearance of the fly. This is especially important in streamer wings, dry fly wings, and tails, but also helpful when gathering body hair for making clipped, hair-bodied flies. To do this, clip the appropriate size bundle of hair close to the skin, then use a small fine-tooth comb to comb out the underfur. Do this several times and from several angles to remove all of the hair. Then place the hair, tip down, into a hair stacker or hair evener. Bang the hair evener hard several times on the fly-tying bench to make the tip ends of the hair even. Carefully remove the hair from the stacker, check to make sure that the hair ends are even enough and then tie in place as required by the fly pattern. Another way do this if you do not have a stacker is to hold the bundle by the cut base, then grab the long ends and pull them free. Relax your grip on the bundle and lay the long hairs on top, with the ends even with the bundle. Repeat this several times until satisfied that most of the tips are even enough for your use.

Step 1 - To make a neat bucktail wing, the tips of the bucktail (or other furs) must be evened so that they are not scraggly like this bundle just cut from the skin.

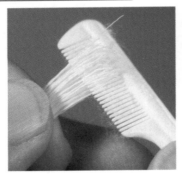

Step 2 - Begin to make neater even strands of fur by using a small comb to remove all of the underfur. This allows the remaining fur to even on the tip ends when placed in a stacker.

Step 3 - Here a stacker is used to even the bucktail. The bucktail has been placed in the stacker, tips down, then the stacker pounded to make the tips even.

Step 4 - Once the bottom cup is removed from the stacker, the even tips can be seen, and the wing tied onto the fly.

TYING TAGS – A tag is a short wrap around the end of the fly just in back of the true body. It is tied before the tail is tied in place, which is tied at the forward end of the tag. Often tags are just a few turns of flat tinsel, but other materials can also be used. To tie in a tag, first tie in the thread forward of the tag, then tie down the tag material. If the tag is tinsel, it is easiest to tie it in at the tie-off point, then wrap the tag tinsel back a turn or two before reversing it and wrapping forward again to tie off with the thread. If using thicker materials, tie in at the rear-most position of the tag, then wrap the thread forward a few turns, followed by the tag material which is then tied off.

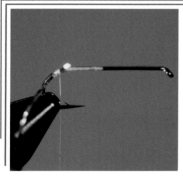

To tie in a tag (often tinsel) first tie down the tag material. Note that tags are often tied a little farther back on the hook shank than other materials.

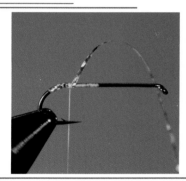

To continue to tie on a tag, wind the thread forward for a few turns and then wrap the tinsel several turns up to this point and tie off with the thread. Often a tail is tied on after this, then the rest of the fly starting with the body.

PALMERING HACKLE – Palmered hackle is hackle that is tied on at the rear of the fly and then spiral-wrapped forward over a previously-wrapped body to make for a buggy, leggy-looking body. The technique can be found in all types of trout flies, but is most typically characteristic of a Woolly Bugger and Woolly Worm. It is also found in some dries and many nymph patterns. The technique, after tying on the tail of the fly, is to tie down a hackle by the tip end in which the hackle fibers have been splayed out at right angles to the main stem. To make sure that the hackle stem will not slip out from under the thread wraps, cut the fibers on each side of the stem for 1/4 inch along the tie-down tip end. This gives the thread something to grip. Next, tie down the fly body and wrap the thread, then the body forward. Secure the body material with thread. At this point, use hackle pliers to grip the end of the palmering hackle and spiral-wrap it forward over the body, tying off at the head or with sufficient space to add any additional materials required by the pattern being tied. If not using rotary pliers, you will have to rotate the hackle pliers once with each turn to prevent the hackle from becoming twisted. If wrapping over chenille, as with a Woolly Bugger, it helps to use the same spiral wrap as used for the chenille so that the palmered hackle can follow in the spaces between the chenille wraps to help protect the hackle. If you do not wish this, then you can tie by counter wrapping the palmering hackle in the opposite direction.

Step 1 - To palmer a fly (spiral wrap hackle around the body) first tie in the hackle to be used, followed by the body, as shown here.

Step 2 - Wrap the thread forward to the tie off point, followed by the body wrap. Here chenille is used for the body.

Step 3 - Begin to palmer the hackle around the body by spiral wrapping it around and up over the body material.

Step 4 - Palmer the hackle up to the tie off point, and tie off with the working thread. Clip any excess hackle and them continue or finish the rest of the fly.

MAKING DUBBING LOOPS AND ADDING DUBBING – Dubbing is chopped and mixed fur and/or synthetics that is spun onto a dubbing loop which in turn is wrapped around the hook shank to make a body. Begin by making a wide loop in the working thread, then tie off this loop with several turns and a half hitch or two around the hook shank. Wax the thread loop with fly-tying wax, spread out the dubbing and twist it in one direction only onto and into the dubbing loop. Use your finger or a dubbing twister to spin the loop to capture the dubbing material between the two threads that make up the loop. Then wrap the working thread forward and out of the way, followed by wrapping the spun dubbing around the hook shank to make the body. Tie off at the forward end of the body with the tying thread.

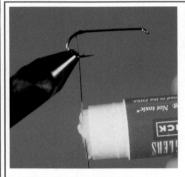

Step 1 - Begin to make a dubbing loop by adding dubbing wax to the thread. Cover a length of thread sufficient to make the loop desired.

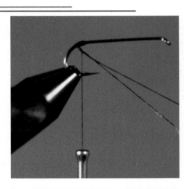

Step 2 - Make a loop of the waxed thread, and then wrap over this loop where it contacts the hook shank. This will secure it for adding the dubbing to the loop.

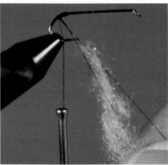

Step 3 - Add the desired dubbing to the loop, positioning it between the two threads that make up the loop. Twist the loop in one direction only to secure the dubbing. Use a dubbing twister or spinner to turn the loop and capture the dubbing between the two strands of the loop.

Step 4 - Wrap the thread forward to the tie off point, leaving the dubbing loop at the tail of the fly for the moment.

Step 5 - Hold the end of the loop with the spinner or hackle pliers and wrap it around the hook shank to form the body as shown here.

Wax the thread loop with fly-tying wax, spread out the dubbing and twist it in one direction only onto and into the dubbing loop.

MAKING MYLAR TUBING BODIES – Some trout streamers are made with Mylar tubing slipped over the hook shank to make the body, rather than wrapping the body material or tinsel around the hook shank. This same technique is possible using plastic translucent tubing materials such as Corsair and E-Z Body. Mylar comes in several sizes and finishes, and always with a thread core. The plastic tubing materials do not have a core, but are available in several sizes and finishes. To use, remove the core from the tubing (Mylar). Then cut the tubing to the length required. If making just the body, make this about the length of the hook shank. If fraying out some of the Mylar to make a tail, then add about 1/4 to 1/3rd the length of the hook. To make a simple body, slip the prepared cut sleeve over the hook shank.

Push the tubing a little to the rear and then tie on the thread in back of the hook eye and clip the excess. Move the tubing back into proper position (slide forward) and then tie down with the working thread. Once the body is complete, tie off and cut the excess thread. Then retie on at the bend of the hook over the tail of the Mylar tubing and tie down, then complete with a whip finish. If making a tail, tie the tail on first, then slide the tubing in place and tie down at the rear before tying off and retying at the head of the fly. Note that in most cases, it is necessary to tie in a wing after tying down the front end of the body. If making a Zonker or Matuka, it is necessary to keep a length of thread at the bend to tie down the rear of the rabbit strip (Zonker) or to thread through the hackle wing (Matuka).

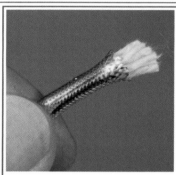

Step 1 - To make a Mylar body streamer fly, first pull the central cord from the Mylar tubing as shown here. The central cord is discarded.

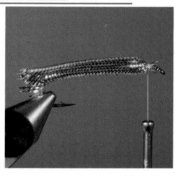

Step 2 - Begin to make a Mylar body trout fly by cutting the tubing to the length of the fly (longer will leave room for a tail of the frayed body material) and then slip the tubing over the body. Tie down the thread in back of the hook eye and then slide the tubing forward to tie down the front end of the tubing with the thread as shown.

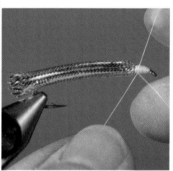

Step 3 - Tie off the head of the fly and the wrapped Mylar body with a whip finish before turning to the tail of the fly.

Step 4 - Tie the thread on again at the tail of the fly to secure the end of the Mylar tubing. Then clip the excess thread before making a whip finish to complete the fly. At this point, the tag end of the thread has yet to be cut.

Step 5 - Once the tail of the fly has been tied off with a whip finish and the thread cut, use a bodkin to fray out the fibers of the Mylar to make a tail. In addition, flies can be tied without this tail and with a previously wrapped tail of other natural and synthetic materials.

If making a tail, tie the tail on first, then slide the tubing in place and tie down at the rear...

MAKING REVERSE TIE MYLAR TUBING BODIES –
Mylar or plastic tubing can also be tied down so that the head tie of the material is hidden. To do this, cut a length of tubing that is about 1-1/4 to 1-1/2 times the length of the hook shank. Remove the core and then tie down, with the length of the Mylar tubing extending in front of the hook (to your right). Once it is securely tied down, tie off with a whip finish and clip the thread. Then use your fingers to roll the tubing back over the hook shank, in essence turning it inside out. Once it is reversed, tie on at the rear of the hook shank and tie down the other end of the tubing. Complete with a whip finish.

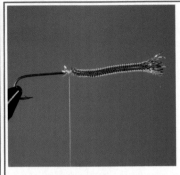

Step 1 - To make a reverse tied Mylar trout streamer, remove the core and cut to length a piece of Mylar as above. Then slip the end of the Mylar over the hook eye with the body extending in front of the hook (to the right). Tie down with thread as shown. Make sure that the thread wrap is immediately in back of the hook eye so that no thread shows when the Mylar is reversed.

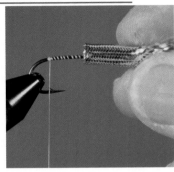

Step 2 - Once the Mylar is tied in place, wind the thread to the bend of the hook and push the Mylar back over itself to turn it inside out and push the Mylar to the rear as shown here.

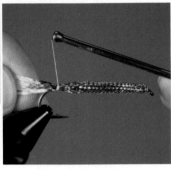

Step 3 - Once the Mylar is pushed to the rear, use the thread to secure the tail of the fly as shown here.

Step 4 - Fray out the Mylar in back of the wrap to make the tail of the fly as shown. Then complete with a whip finish.

ADDING EYES TO STREAMERS – Eyes can be added to streamers in a number of ways. To add painted eyes, first completely finish the head of the fly with several coats of head cement. Then use small bottles of enamel paint (Testors is good) to make the eyes. Shake the bottle, then remove the cap and work from the small amount of paint on the inside of the cap. For a tool, use two sizes of pinheads or finishing nails. Use the larger of the two for making the eye color of white, yellow or another light color. Dot on each side of the head of the fly and allow to cure. Once cured, use the smaller of the pins or nails (or a pin or nail with the head cut off and smoothed) to make a smaller pupil of black, red or another dark color. Commercially available eye painting tools are available if you do not wish to make your own. It is also possible to add painted eyes to the shoulder of streamers. To do this, coat the shoulder with a layer or two of head cement, then repeat as above to add the eye and the pupil to the fly. To add prism eyes, select the right size eye for your fly, peel from the backing and add to each side of the fly head. Tip – to make this easier, crease the eye through the center before removing it from the backing so that the eye more readily conforms to the rounded shape of the head. Once the eyes are in place, coat with several layers of head cement or a single layer of epoxy to keep the eye from falling off. To add plastic or rattling doll eyes, use a small dot of glue in the back of the eye to glue the eye to the head of the fly. If necessary, coat with head cement or epoxy.

Add painted eyes to streamer flies by using a nail head or pin head to dip into paint and form the basic eye form in a color contrasting to the fly head.

Use a smaller nail or pinhead dipped into a contrasting paint to dot the eye and make the pupil of the eye on the fly.

TYING DUMBBELL/HOURGLASS EYES - Dumbbell and hourglass eyes have revolutionized fly-fishing deep for all manner of fish, including trout. They are typically used on Clousers or when making streamer-like minnow imitations to fish the bottom of deep pools or to get down in a fast riffle. To tie them down, first make a series of wraps around the hook shank and the center of the eye. This will place the eye cockeyed, but this is OK since it will allow you to get a tight wrap on the eye. With the eye canted at an angle, (I position it so that the eye on the far side of the hook is canted forward) take your fingernail and pull the eye back into a right angle alignment with the hook shank. Then wrap over the hook shank and eye to hold the eye in this position. This creates tension in the first series of wraps to help hold the eye down and in the proper position. It is also possible to make other figure-8 patterns with the thread – going around the eye on each side and under the hook shank or building up a wrap by going around the stem of the wrap between the eye and the hook shank. If desired, add a drop of CA glue (any brand of the super glues) or a drop of epoxy to the eye at this point to secure it. For most weighted flies, it helps to use a hook with a turned-down eye and place the hook point down in the vise to tie the eyes on the shank. Place the fly in the vise hook point up to tie the fly. The eye in this position with a turned-down eye hook (which will ride up when fished) makes the fly almost weedless on the bottom.

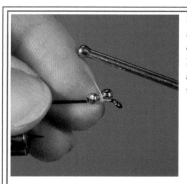

Step 1 - To tie in dumb bell eyes on a fly such as a Clouser, wrap over the eye and the hook shank as shown. Note that initially the eye will be at an angle to the hook shank, rather than at 90 degrees to the shank.

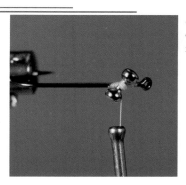

Step 2 - The angle of the dumb bell eye will change once a cross wrap is made over the eyes.

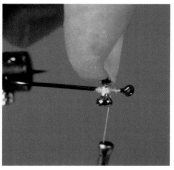

Step 3 - To straighten the eyes on the hook shank, use your fingernail or thumbnail to pull back on the forward part of the eyes and then wrap over in the other direction with the tying thread.

This creates tension in the first series of wraps to help hold the eye down and in the proper position.

ADDING BEADS AND CONE HEADS – Bead-head and cone-head flies have become very popular in recent years. The bead on the front of the fly – directly in back of the hook eye – adds weight and color or flash that makes it very attractive to fish. Beads and cone heads come in a number of sizes, finishes and colors and are sold by all fly-tying outlets. They are also available from craft stores, although here you will have to guess the size for the hooks that you are using, or take along a hook to test the beads in the store. Unfortunately, since hooks come with different shape hook bends, gaps and wire sizes, even in a given standard "size," it is difficult to make more than general estimates as to which bead will fit on which hook. Ideally, you want a bead that will slide onto the point of the hook (with the barb bent down) and slide around the bend to seat against the back of the hook eye. With the bead in place the eye must still be exposed for adding the leader tippet. Usually, the thread is tied down in back of and after the bead or beads are positioned on the hook. With some flies, beads are also added subsequently as part, or all, of the body. In these cases, the beads are added all at once, with the thread then added and the rest of the fly tied around these beads. A tip here is to use Model Perfect or round bend hooks when tying bead-head flies, since the sharper bends in Limerick, O'Shaughnessy and other hook styles limits the size of the beads which will easily slide onto the hook.

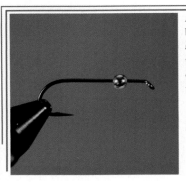

Add cones or beads to hooks by first bending down the bend of the hook and sliding the bead or cone over the hook and onto the shank. Perfect or round bend hooks are best for this.

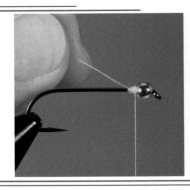

To position the bead or cone on the hook, begin the thread in back of the bead and wrap a bump of thread to hold the bead or cone in place as shown here.

ADDING SHEET LEAD AND WEIGHT TO FLIES – Self-adhesive backed sheet lead or soft metal can be added to a hook to make flattened nymph bodies as well as the beer-belly shape of Zonkers. To add this to a fly when making a streamer, first cut the metal to make it the length desired (hook shank length or slightly shorter) and double the width desired in the underbody. Fold the tape in half before removing the backing, then remove the backing, position the hook between the folded metal like a sandwich, and squeeze with pliers to hold on the hook. For nymphs, the metal body will be flat - at right angles to the hook plane. Then use your coarse scissors to trim and taper the metal body to shape. Tie on the thread and wrap the body with thread from one end to the other and tie off. To secure the wrap, coat with head cement, or better still, thinned epoxy or CA glue. Then tie the thread back on and tie the fly using standard fly-tying materials. To make a Zonker body, use the same method to measure and fold the metal. In this case, the metal body will be in the same plane as the hook, and the hook shank will be placed at the fold in the metal. Remove the backing, position the hook shank against the fold and squeeze with pliers. Use coarse scissors to trim the ends to a belly shape. You can wrap the metal with thread as with nymph bodies or leave it bare, since it will be covered with the Mylar tubing to make the Zonker. In both cases, it is best to make up a number of these hooks with body forms in advance, ready to tie.

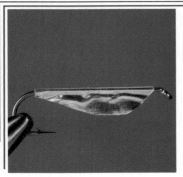

Add sheet lead to flies to make Zonkers or nymphs by using the self-adhesive lead taper made for this purpose. To do this, fold and cut the tape into the size and shape desired for the hook, them remove the backing and fold onto the hook as shown. Mylar tubing will go over this body.

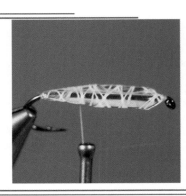

Tape can also be folded and cut to make flattened nymph bodies using the same techniques as above. The lead sheet is positioned at right angles to the hook shank, rather than in line with it as with a Zonker pattern.

ADDING LEAD – Lead and lead substitutes are used for weighting streamers, wet flies and nymphs. Note that while we will use the term lead throughout, lead substitutes are available and there are areas and states (California for one) that have regulations controlling the sale and use of lead. Lead and lead wire substitutes are available in different diameters, ranging from about 0. 010 inch to 0. 035 inch. In addition, weighted materials are available in flat sheets and tape. Lead can be added to flies in a number of ways. The simplest way is to wrap the lead around the hook shank, then tie on the thread and wrap over this, with spiral criss-cross wrappings to secure the lead. It is also best to make a small tapering "ramp" at each end of the lead wrap for smoothly adding tapered body materials. Lead can be wrapped over the entire hook shank, just at the tail end or just at the head end.

These latter two methods – particularly the wrap on the head end — will give the fly a jerky, up/down movement with any twitchy retrieve. This is particularly attractive to fish. Another way to add lead is to cut strips slightly shorter than the shank length, position them parallel to the shank and wrap over them to secure them. Usually two are added, one on each side of the hook shank to help simulate the flattened body of many nymphs. Additional lead can be added by using three or four strips, spacing them parallel to the hook shank and equidistant around the shank. If tying a fly with a white or light colored body, be sure to add a coat of head cement to the lead before going further to prevent the lead from bleeding through and discoloring the light body. This is not usually necessary if tying bodies of dark gray, brown, olive or black.

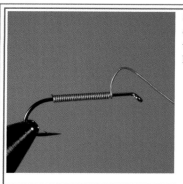

Step 1 - One way to wrap lead wire onto a hook shank is to make tight wraps around the hook as shown here. Any excess lead can be cut off.

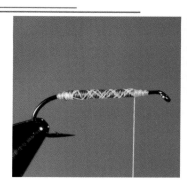

Step 2 - To secure the lead on the hook, wrap over it with thread as shown and make a small "ramp" of thread at each end to taper the body material that will subsequently be added.

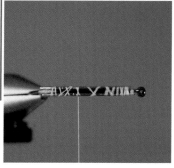

Step 3 - One other way to add lead to a hook shank is to cut two lengths equal to the shank length and wrap them in place on each side of the hook shank.

Lead can be wrapped over the entire hook shank, just at the tail end or just at the head end.

TYING OVER LEAD - If tying over lead with floss, it is best to first make an underwrap of thin yarn, or to use enough floss to smooth out the gaps and ridges formed by the lead wire. A sealer coat is also best over any lead wrap to prevent the lead from bleeding through and discoloring the fly body.

TYING FOAM BODIES – Foam is not used widely in trout flies, except for the closed-cell foam (will not absorb water) used for terrestrials such as ants, beetles, jassids, hoppers, crickets, lady bugs and the like. Open-cell foam, which will absorb water, is used for some nymph patterns both as a body and underbody. Foam is available in several forms, including round cylinders, sheet foam, strips (cut sheets) and shaped foam. Strip or sheet foam is widely used for nymphs, wrapping it around the hook shank to form the body. It can be used the same way for terrestrials. In both cases, the foam is tied on as a standard body material and wrapped around, then tied off to form a body or underbody.

Round cylinder foam (closed-cell) is usually prepared as a short cylinder and tied on at the center of the hook shank and center of the foam cylinder to make flies such as a foam McMurray Ant and similar bees and wasps. Cylinder foam makes great cricket or hopper bodies by tying on at the one end of the foam and in back of the hook eye. Strip foam or strips cut from sheet foam can also be tied on at the rear of a hook shank and then folded over to the make a beetle body or segmented parts of an ant. Foam is a versatile material for making many flies, and far more adaptable when making floating panfish and bass bugs and saltwater flies.

Step 1 - One way to make a simple foam body for a beetle is to tie in the thread at the rear of the hook, then tie down a strip of closed cell foam as shown. Then wrap the thread forward to tie down the foam when it is folded over the make the body.

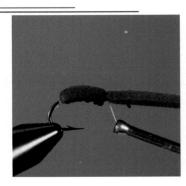

Step 2 - Make the foam body of the beetle by folding over the foam and then tying it into place with the tying thread as shown here.

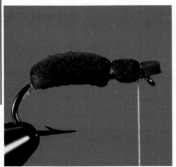

Step 3 - Wrap the thread forward again and then tie off the foam to make the thorax . To make the complete beetle, legs of deer hair, hackle or synthetics would be added to the beetle between the previous step and this step.

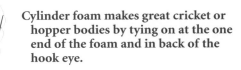

Cylinder foam makes great cricket or hopper bodies by tying on at the one end of the foam and in back of the hook eye.

TYING STREAMER HAIR WINGS – Traditional streamer wings such as those for Mickey Finn and similar patterns involve bucktail tied directly on top of the hook shank and directly in back of the hook eye. Wings are added after adding all other materials such as the body and ribbing. Wings can be added before or after adding a throat. To add a bucktail wing, first clip the bucktail from the skin, and use a small comb to remove any underfur. Then place the wing material, tip down, into a stacker or evener. Tap several times and remove the wing, which should now have the tip ends approximately even. Trim the butt ends relative to the length needed for the fly wing. Position the wing over the head of the fly, taking care that the length of the wing is proportional to the fly and hook size. Generally, a wing of about 1-1/4 to 1-

1/2 times the length of the hook shank is standard. Use the soft-loop method to get the wing on straight and securely. Hold the wing in place with your left hand, bring the thread straight up on the near side of the hook, then pinch the thread with your left thumb and index finger. Holding the thread and the wing, pull the thread straight down in back of the hook, and pull down to capture the thread. Repeat. Trim any excess wing material in front of the wrap, tapering it to correspond with the final shape of the tapered head. Complete more thread wraps to cover the wing butts and prepare the head for finishing. This method will assure that the wing will be tied correctly and straight on top of the hook shank.

To make a bucktail streamer wing, first comb out the fur as shown to remove all underfur and then stack to make the tips even.

Place the bucktail in position on top of the hook shank and use the soft loop method to secure the bucktail. Then clip the forward ends of the fur as shown before completing the head.

STACKING HAIR WINGS FOR STREAMERS - Some streamers have stacked wings of different colors of bucktail. An example is the Mickey Finn, with a wing of alternating yellow/red/yellow bucktail. To tie this, first add the base wing of yellow, following the directions above. Then repeat with a smaller bundle of red, again following the above directions to place the red directly on top of the yellow wing. Then finally add a final top wing of yellow over the red, again following the directions as above. When complete, the three parts of the wing should be separated by color and look the same on both sides of the fly.

Step 1 - To stack a hair wing as when making a Mickey Finn streamer fly, repeat the above step with a second color of bucktail to place this second color directly on top of the first as shown here for making a Mickey Finn.

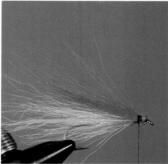

Step 2 - Clip the forward part of the added wing material as shown before stacking more wing material.

Step 3 - To complete a stacked fly such as a Mickey Finn, add the third layer of stacked wing material – in this case another layer of yellow bucktail on top of the two stacked layers of yellow and red. Trim the forward part of the bucktail and then complete the fly by wrapping the head.

...first add the base wing of yellow...

TYING STREAMER HACKLE WINGS – Saddle hackle – that is long hackle feathers – is used for many streamer wings for trout and can be found in patterns like the Black Ghost, Gray Ghost and others. To tie these wings, you will need hackle matched by width, shape and length. For most flies you will use two pair – two hackle feathers on each side. All hackle feathers have a natural curve to them or concave and convex sides. Match the feathers so that the concave side (dull side) of each feather faces the middle of the fly. Measure the feathers for length, making the wing about 1-1/2 times the length of the hook shank, or follow specific pattern instructions. Cut off the excess feather at the butt end and then cut the fibers back about 1/4 inch on each side of the main feather stem. This creates some "tooth" to the main

stem for more secure wrapping. Place the entire wing with the feathers on top of the hook shank, with the feathers parallel to the hook shank and the plane of the feathers parallel to the hook plane. The thread must be back far enough from the hook eye to allow proper tying of the wing. Then bring the thread straight up on the near side of the hook with your right hand, pinch the thread and the feathers with your left thumb and index finger, then pull the thread straight down on the far side of the hook. Pull tight and repeat. Then trim any excess feather stems. Add any topping (if used) at this time. Then continue wrapping with thread to build up a smooth and uniform head. A common alternative method is to tie the wings concave side out so they will flare and pulse in the water.

To make a streamer wing of saddle hackle feathers, first choose two pairs of hackle feathers that are equal in appearance, length and width. Then position them with one pair as each side of the wing. Usually wings are made so that the two pairs are concave side out as shown, so that the wings will flare and pulse in the water on retrieve.

To complete the streamer hackle wing, position the wing hackles on top of the hook shank and tie in using the soft loop method. This will assure that the wings stay on top and are not flared to one side or twisted. Wing length can vary from about 1-1/4 to 2 times the hook shank length.

TYING SYNTHETIC WING MATERIAL FOR STREAMERS – Synthetic materials can be used in place of natural fur on streamer wings, or added to the natural materials in some flies. Examples would be using materials such as Unique, Super Hair, Ultra Hair and others for the wings of flies, or adding materials such as Krystal Flash, Crystal Splash or Flashabou to add flash and sparkle to the natural or synthetic wings. To use the synthetics, clip and tie in place just as you would the natural material. In many sizes, the synthetics are more slippery than natural materials, so use the soft loop to position the wing and make tight wraps to hold it. If making a thick wing, it often helps to add several small bundles rather than one large initial bundle. Another tip is to trim the tail ends of the synthetic fibers. Since

synthetics do not taper as do natural furs, you can get a more tapered look by thinning the end of the wing. Do this by selectively cutting using standard scissors, although a quicker and easier way is to use a pair of barber's thinning scissors that have one toothed blade. Special fly-tying thinning scissors are also available. Flash materials such as Krystal Flash, Crystal Splash and Flashabou supplement the look of the fly when added to the wing. For this, the best solution is to cut two small bundles and tie in one on each side of the fly after the wing has been added and secured. An alternative to this is to cut a long bundle, tie it in at the halfway point on one side of the fly, and then bring the long end around the head of the fly to the opposite side. Then continue wrapping to secure the flash material on that side in place.

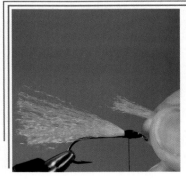

Tie in synthetic wing material the same way that you tie in bucktail, using the soft loop Method to keep the wing material on top of the hook shank as shown here. Finish by clipping the excess synthetic and then wrap the head to complete the fly.

...cut two small bundles and tie in one on each side of the fly after the wing has been added...

TYING TOPPING OVER STREAMER WINGS –
Topping over streamer wings is typically peacock herl, but can be other materials including ostrich, synthetics, bucktail, etc. This is simply held in place over the previously tied wing with the thread in the same position as when first tying the wing in place. Then, just as with a wing, bring the thread straight up on the near side of the hook, pinch the thread and the topping with your left index finger and thumb, and bring the thread down on the far side of the hook shank. Pull tight, repeat two or more times, then trim the excess topping and wrap with thread to complete a uniform head.

Topping of peacock herl, other colors of wing materials or synthetics can be added to any streamer fly to make the fly look more natural and like the dark-shaded natural minnow it imitates. To do this, use the soft loop method to tie down the topping once the rest of the wing has been completed. Peacock herl is being added here.

...bring the thread straight up on the near side of the hook...

HANDLING MARABOU – Marabou wings are great on simple trout streamer flies, in such patterns as white, yellow and black marabou with a silver tinsel body. But because of its fluffy nature, handling marabou is often difficult. The best way that I have found is to first carefully cut the marabou from the stem of the feather, cutting as close to the stem as possible. You can then pull this strip of material away and fold it over several times to make a bundle for tying. To keep the marabou from floating around and interfering with the tying process, wet your fingers and smooth back the marabou. Do this as needed to slightly moisten the marabou to keep it in place. Do not moisten the area where you will be tying the marabou in place, since this may not allow complete penetration of the head cement when you finish the fly. It is also possible to dip the marabou (all except the end to be tied) into water to moisten it and make it easy to handle. Other tyers like spraying it with static-preventing sprays used for ironing and clothing.

Fluffy marabou or the similar chickabou is difficult to handle and tie down properly. One tip to doing this is to lightly moisten the marabou wing material so that it will straight out and be easier to handle. Here, fluffy marabou is held over top of the moistened marabou, which has been easily tied to a hook shank.

...slightly moisten the marabou to keep it in place.

TAPERING BODIES - Natural insects and minnows have basic tapered shapes, thicker in the middle than they are at the tail end. So should flies. This is easy to do by controlling your body materials when wrapping. One method for wet flies, dry flies and nymphs is to tie down and begin the wrap in the middle of the hook shank where you want the body to be the thickest. Then wrap forward to the head of the fly, back to the tail and then back up over the previous wraps to tie off at the head. This makes for three layers of wrap over the forward part of the fly and two layers of wrap over the rear of the fly. An alternative method is to lay down a base of thread built up to the shape of the body that you desire, and then overwrap it once with the final body material. It is also possible to adjust the amount of material being laid down by how close you make each turn of material to the previous wrap. Controlling the twist or tightness of body material is another way to control body thickness. Floss can be twisted to make a tight bundle and thick wrap or untwisted to make a thin, almost ribbon-like layer for a thinner body or to taper a body. Similarly, twisted materials such as yarn or other body material can be twisted or untwisted to control the amount of material being added.

TYING COMPARADUN "HACKLE" – Comparaduns are those flies which do not use a traditional hackle and which do not rest on the tips of any hackle as do traditional Catskill dry flies. Instead, they float on the surface film as do the natural dun mayflies when first emerging from their nymphal form, and have a deer hair "hackle" or wing that makes a half circle on top of the fly. They also have the wing or hackle a little farther back than on traditional flies, more like the thorax ties developed by Vince Marinaro in the 1940s. To make this, choose and prepare (clip, comb and stack) a small bundle of deer hair, appropriate in type and bundle size for the fly being tied. Then hold the bundle, tips facing forward, over the hook shank at about the 1/3rd position back from the hook eye and wrap down with tying thread. For this, you must use the soft loop previously described. When doing this, hold the deer hair in place as you tighten the thread so that the deer hair maintains position on top of the hook shank. Pull tight, then bring the thread forward of the bundle and wrap a bump sufficient to raise the deer hair to a vertical position. Also, position the deer hair fibers as you do this. When viewed from the end, you want the deer hair in a 160- to 180-degree arc and to be completely on the upper part of the fly – nothing below the hook shank. Then tie the rest of the fly by wrapping the tail in place, adding the body and tying off.

Step 1 - To tie in a Comparadun deer-hair hackle, first clip, comb and position the bundle of deer hair over the hook shank as shown, with the tips facing forward.

Step 2 - Continue to make the Comparadun fly by making two loops with the thread using the soft loop method and then pull down on the thread to flare and raise the deer hair.

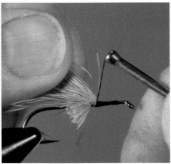

Step 3 - Wrap thread in front of the bundle to raise the deer-hair hackle to a vertical upright position as shown. Done properly, the hackle should be vertical and should make a 160- to 180-degree arc, side to side.

Step 4 - Here a Comparadun hackle is shown from the front of the fly, to show the arc that the deer-hair hackle makes when complete.

TYING SPEY OR SOFT HACKLE WET FLY COLLARS
Soft-hackle wet flies are old patterns that are still very effective for trout. The hackle used is softer hen hackle and often tied slightly longer than standard wet fly collar hackle. Tie these the same way, by tying in the butt end, then wrapping the hackle around the hook shank.

MARRYING QUILL WING SECTIONS – Some flies, such as the Parmachene Belle, have married wings. This means that the quill section wing is made up of two or more different sections, each of different colors. This takes advantage of the natural locking mechanism of the wing fibers that occurs on any quill and which is evident in any quill feather. To make a married wing, cut out appropriate sizes of the sections of matched quills to make the married wing. Usually this will be about 1/2 to 1/3rd of the normal quill wing width. Then hold the two parts together by the edge and stroke them while bending them slightly from side to side. This bending helps to lock the two different color sections together. Once each of the wings is "married" then join the two wings and tie them into place using standard wing-tying procedures.

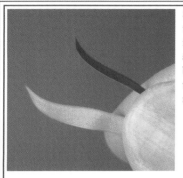

Step 1 - To marry sections of quill together to make a multicolored wet fly wing, first choose the quill sections to be used. Two pairs must be used for each side of the fly and the different color quill sections must match in length and curvature.

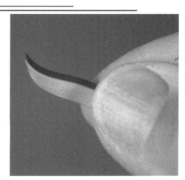

Step 2 - Marry the sections of quill by placing them together and them stroking them back while slightly wiggling them from side to side to get the fibers of the two different sections to lock together.

Step 3 - The completed wing of married quill section will look like this on a hook after the wing is tied down and before the forward part of the quills are clipped and the head wrapped. This wing consists of three sections – yellow/red/yellow and is shown without the rest of the fly.

This takes advantage of the natural locking mechanism of the wing fibers...

TYING REVERSED-WING BULLET HEADS – This method, first used by turn-of-the-century fly-tier Carrie Stevens and later popularized by Keith Fulsher with his Thunder Creek series of flies, uses a reverse tie of the wing to make a bullet head. The method is simple. After tying on the rest of the fly (tail, body, ribbing) tie in a wing of bucktail (which is most common, but other materials can be used) with the tips facing forward rather than back over the body. Also, tie this so that the wing (which extends to the right of the fly) surrounds the hook shank. After tying this wing on, wrap the thread back to a point about 1/3rd the way back from the hook eye, or to a position where you want the head

secured. Then fold the wing back over the tie-down point so that the wing surrounds the hook shank and body. Use the tying thread to tie down the wing and secure it with a whip finish, then seal with head cement. This type of bullet head and wing can be made full or very sparse. It can also be made in two parts, with a dark top and light bottom, with the two parts pulled back to make the typical light belly/dark back camouflage of a minnow. Most flies are finished with a painted or prism eye added to the bullet head. A final possibility is to use red thread so that the wrap to hold the head in place looks like a red gill on the fly.

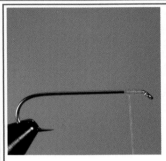

Step 1 - To make a bullet-head streamer (Keith Fulsher Thunder Creek series or Carrie Stevens style) you must first tie the tail, body and ribbing of the fly before adding the head. Here, the method is shown with the thread tied down without the rest of the fly in place.

Step 2 - Clip, comb, even and prepare a length of bucktail and then tie in place using the soft-loop method with the tips facing forward in front of the fly. One difference in the tying here is that when making a fly with only one head color, the bucktail is tied so that it will surround the hook shank, rather than staying on one side of it. If using two different color materials to make a dark top and light bottom, then each material is tied so that it will stay on one side of the hook shank. After any of these steps, wrap the thread back a few turns until positioned properly to tie off the head when it is folded back.

Step 3 - After the bucktail is tied in place, use your fingers or a flaring tube to reverse the bucktail on itself and to fold it over the rest of the fly and the hook as shown here

Step 4 - Complete the head of a Thunder Creek style bucktail streamer by using the working thread to wrap over the bucktail and tie it down. Finish with a whip finish and clip the excess thread.

TAPERING HEADS – To make for a neat fly, the head must be tapered. This is important in all flies, but most important in streamers and bucktails that have a longer and more noticeable head. Often other fly-tyers will judge the quality of your tying ability by the shape of the head. To make a tapered head, you must clip and trim the materials under the head to the same general shape. On streamers this means that you must taper the wing and throat materials after tying them in place but before making wraps to completely cover the butts of the wing material. Do this with scissors, paying

attention to both sides of the fly. Once the materials are trimmed, complete the head by wrapping evenly over the head with the thread to completely cover the underlying materials and to smooth the head. Since streamers are often tied with heavier thread than for other flies, some tyers like to tie off (whip finish) the working thread, and then tie on with a very fine thread that will fill in the spaces between the heavier thread and make the wrap appear more smooth. In theory this is fine, but in practice, the head cement or epoxy finish will make any wrap appear smooth.

Chapter 4

One Hundred Top Trout Patterns

The following list of 100 top trout flies is bound to provoke arguments. There are many reasons for the selections listed. One is the fact that we wanted to include the best possible flies for all trout, through all seasons, on any waters, in any part of the country. Obviously, no fly will do it all. Dry flies will not work when the trout are holding on the bottom and grubbing nymphs. Bottom-fished nymphs will not work if the trout are in feeding lanes and gorging on Tricos floating downstream. Neither may work if you are after a big cannibalistic brown chasing sculpins through a deep pool. Then too, there are Western patterns that are not designed for Eastern fishing, and vice versa. Examples of each are the Adams, Light Cahill and Edson Tiger Light – principally Eastern flies - San Juan Worm, Egg-Sucking Leech and salmon fly nymph patterns of Western waters.

In addition, there are no exact patterns or recipes for each fly, even though for the original pattern the inventor might have had only one design and choice of materials in mind. Examples are the changes of the popular Adams from the original spent-wing design to one with a hackle-tip wing to those tied today that commonly are tied with an upright divided wing using hackle fibers or the increasingly-popular parachute style. Also, new hooks, materials, thread strengths and sizes, synthetics and hackle improvements have also caused slight to radical evolutions of fly patterns over the years. This means that you have a lot of choices in tying any of the following in terms of hooks, thread and materials, if not the basic pattern.

Some thoughts on all this are as follows:

HOOKS – Hook styles and suggested sizes are listed for each pattern. In most cases, you can select the hook manufacturer of your choice. Also, suggested sizes are just suggestions – assuming the materials are available, you can obviously tie flies larger or smaller than those listed. In most cases, you can get by fine with your favorite dry fly hook for the dry patterns (perhaps a light wire hook, 1 or 2X long). Similarly, you will do fine with a regular length standard weight wet fly hook for wet flies and a weighted 2X to 3X long nymph hook for most nymphs. For specialty patterns such as the curved sow bugs, scuds, and some nymph patterns there are special curved shank hooks, just as there are for swimming nymphs with the upward bent hooks. For streamers choose something between a 2X- and 4X-long shank hook, unless tying some of the classic Carrie Stevens Northeast streamer patterns or examples of trolling streamers. If trying to get a close match to a particular hook, check out *HOOKS FOR THE FLY*, by William E. Schmidt, a thorough cross-reference for hooks from all major manufacturers. (Note - Complete information on all books listed can be found in the Bibliography.)

THREAD – Threads for these patterns are listed as to color only. Color of thread is particularly important not only in determining the color of the head of the fly, but also in the body color of some flies. This is particularly important in flies with translucent body materials or fur dubbing where the thread color might show through to either match the dubbing/body material or contrast with it. Thread size is not listed since the thread size will vary with the fly or hook size, and most patterns can be tied in a wide range of sizes. Standard thread size for trout flies might be considered 6/0 for sizes 10 through 14, 8/0 for smaller sizes and 4/0 for larger size nymphs and streamers. In addition, many tyers develop a brand loyalty to a particular thread, and substitutes are usually quite acceptable.

HACKLE – Hackle has improved greatly over the years, with quality, variety, colors and length of hackle feathers all better than those available to tyers of the past. Beginning with Metz and rapidly followed by companies such as Whiting, AuSable, Bob's Hackle Farm, Collins', Ewing, Hobbs, Hoffman, Hurst, Imperial, Keough, Minnesota, Spencer's, and others, all hackle producers have produced better and more refined hackle and maintained better quality control. While picking hackle as to quality and dry fly/wet fly type is somewhat subjective, many companies are now grading hackle as to overall quality.

In most cases, only the shade of the hackle is noted in the following patterns, although obviously different sizes and types of hackle will be necessary for different sizes of flies. For more information, check one of the several books on fly-tying materials or the specialty book, *THE METZ BOOK OF HACKLE*, by Eric Leiser.

MATERIALS – While once there were only natural furs and feathers along with wool chenilles, silk flosses and metallic tinsels, today there is a wide range of synthetics. Synthetics are widely used in all parts of the fly, including tails, bodies, wings, wing cases on nymphs, ribbing, etc. You can find Mylar tinsels, Antron yarn and stranded flash for streamers, synthetic legs and wing cases for nymphs and man-made body materials and tails for dry flies. As a result of the wide range of natural and synthetic materials available, substitutions are readily possible between materials of the same color and general type. Switching to a synthetic dubbing in place of floss will not retain the same appearance of the fly, even though the "new" fly pattern might work well and take lots of trout. Changing a natural dubbing mix for a same-color synthetic closely resembling the original might work fine, even if subtle changes are apparent in the finished fly.

For more information on the many materials available, consult *MODERN FLY-TYING MATERIALS*, by Dick Talleur; *FLY-TYING MATERIALS*, by Eric Leiser; and *FLY-DRESSING MATERIALS*, by John Veniard.

Fly Patterns

Dry Flies
ADAMS
MARCH BROWN
LIGHT CAHILL
NO-HACKLE PALE MORNING DUN
IRRESISTIBLE
QUILL GORDON
BROWN BIVISIBLE
HENDRICKSON
MOSQUITO
BLUE-WINGED OLIVE
RED QUILL
GRAY FOX
GINGER QUILL
BLACK GNAT
GREEN DRAKE THORAX
LOOPWING DUN
CAENIS SPINNER
BROWN DRAKE SPINNER
GREEN DRAKE EXTENDED-BODY
   MAYFLY
HAYSTACK
STIMULATOR
RENEGADE
DANCING CADDIS
HUMPY
DUN VARIANT
PALE MORNING DUN
PARACHUTE ADAMS
GRIFFITH'S GNAT
ROYAL WULFF
GODDARD CADDIS
LIME TRUDE
ELK HAIR CADDIS
COMPARADUN
DARBEE TWO-FEATHER MAYFLY

Wet Flies
BLACK GNAT
GRAY NYMPH
LIGHT CAHILL
DARK CAHILL
LEADWING COACHMAN
COWDUNG
ALDER
PROFESSOR
PARTRIDGE AND GREEN
GRIZZLY KING
MONTREAL
PICKET PIN
PARMACHENE BELLE
WOODCOCK AND ORANGE
McGINTY

Nymphs
GOLD-RIBBED HARE'S EAR
PHEASANT TAIL NYMPH
BITCH CREEK NYMPH
BEAD-HEAD PRINCE
OLIVE BEAD-HEAD SCUD
SERENDIPITY
BROOKS' MONTANA STONEFLY
OLIVE CADDIS
SAND CASE CADDIS
BRASSIE
TEENY NYMPH
HEATHEN
BREADCRUST
NEWBORN CADDIS
CADDIS PUPA
CDC EMERGER, OLIVE
FLEDERMOUSE
COMPARADUN EMERGER (A.K.A.
   COMPARAEMERGER)
DEEP SPARKLE PUPA

Streamers
MUDDLER MINNOW
BLACK-NOSE DACE
MICKEY FINN
WHITE MARABOU STREAMER
EMERALD SHINER – THUNDER
   CREEK SERIES
NINE-THREE
GRAY GHOST
BLACK GHOST
LITTLE BROOK TROUT
EDSON TIGER DARK
EDSON TIGER LIGHT
SUPER STREAKER
CLOUSER MINNOW
ZONKER
MATUKA, OLIVE
MYLAR MINNOW
SPRUCE FLY – LIGHT

Terrestrials
McMURRAY ANT
DEER HAIR INCHWORM
LETORT HOPPER
LETORT CRICKET
JASSID
FOAM JAPANESE BEETLE
RED ANT
DAMSELFLY

Miscellaneous
MADAME X
NEVERSINK SKATER
HORNBERG
EGG-SUCKING LEECH
SAN JUAN WORM
WOOLLY BUGGER
GLO BUG

Dry Flies

ADAMS

A basic dry fly that is a must for any angler's box.

This basic dry fly is a staple of any fly-fisherman's box. Reports indicate that it was developed by Leonard Halladay of Mayfield, MI and first used by Charles F. Adams in 1922. It was named for Adams as a result of his great success with the fly when fishing Michigan's Broadman River. According to fly-tyer, writer, and historian Eric Leiser, it was first tied as a spent wing. It is now more popularly tied with a hackle-tip wing (as illustrated here), divided upright wing fly, or as a parachute.

Tied by Chuck Edghill.

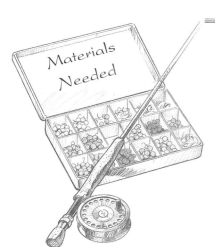

Hook – Standard dry fly hook in sizes 12 to 16.
Thread – Gray or black, appropriate to the size of the fly.
Tail – Mixed grizzly and brown hackle
Body – Gray muskrat dubbing fur
Wings - Grizzly hackle tips, upright and divided
Hackle – Mixed grizzly and brown

Tying sequence:

1. Tie in the thread on the hook shank about 1/3rd back from the hook eye.
2. Tie in the wings (hackle tips) facing forward, clip the excess butt ends, then wrap around the base to raise the hackle tips to an upright position.
3. Use the thread to separate (divide) the two hackle-tip wings keeping them upright.
4. Wrap the thread to the tail and tie the tail.
5. Tie in the body material of gray dubbing after positioning the thread between the tail and the wings or prepare the dubbing on the waxed tying thread.
6. Wrap the thread to a position just in back of the wings. (Only if using separate dubbing material or dubbing on a separate thread.)
7. Wrap the dubbing body down to the tail, then up and down the hook shank to build up the body as desired before tying off in back of the wings.
8. Pull any excess body material off of the tying thread. If tied onto a separate thread, clip the excess thread (but NOT the tying thread!).
9. Tie in the hackle feathers of brown and grizzly and wind first one then the second both in front and in back of the wings. Tie off and clip the excess hackle.
10. Hold the hackle tip wings after wrapping the hackle in place and use the other hand to wrap the thread through the hackle to help secure it.
11. Clip the excess hackle.
12. Finish the fly by making a small head of tying thread, then whip finish the head and clip the excess thread.
13. Seal with head cement

MARCH BROWN, OR AMERICAN MARCH BROWN

A dry fly for early-season fishing, with several different versions available.

This fly is an example of a dressing by Preston Jennings, a seminal fly-fisherman and author of *A BOOK OF TROUT FLIES*, first published in 1935. It is considered the standard fly for both Eastern and Western March Brown Mayfly hatches, though it was developed and fished primarily in the East. It is a basic fly for early season fishing on most streams. It is generally a large mayfly, leading to gulping takes by trout much of the time.

Tied by Chuck Edghill.

Hook – Standard dry fly hook, sizes 10 to 16
Thread – Orange or brown
Tail – Dark brown hackle fibers
Body – Dubbing of red fox belly mixed with sandy fur from hare's ear (tan rabbit dubbing an optional dressing)
Wings – Wood duck flank feathers, upright and divided
Hackle – Brown and grizzly or dun and grizzly (original dressing)

Tying sequence:

1. Tie in the thread on the hook shank about 1/3rd back from the hook eye. Clip the excess thread.
2. Tie in the wood duck wings facing forward, then use wraps of thread to raise the wings to an upright position. Divide them also with thread.
3. Wrap the thread towards the bend of the hook and tie in the tail fibers.
4. Return the thread to the midpoint of the hook shank and tie in the dubbing material, or secure the dubbing to the waxed tying thread.
5. Wrap the tying thread forward to just in back of the wings. (Only if the dubbing is separate from the tying thread.)
6. Wrap the dubbing material up and down the hook shank to form a tapered body, then tie off with the tying thread. Clip or remove any excess dubbing material.
7. Tie in the hackle with the tying thread and clip any excess hackle.
8. Wind the hackle around the hook shank in front of and in back of the wings. Tie off with the thread after winding several turns of thread through the hackle to reinforce it. Clip the excess hackle.
9. Make sure that the hackle and wings are out of the way, and finish a small head. Tie off with a whip finish.
10. Seal with head cement.

LIGHT CAHILL

A standard dry fly that is easy to tie and effective to use.

The Light Cahill is another standard dry fly that is a must for any fly box. This fly is a light cream/sulfur color that closely imitates any of the Eastern sulfur mayfly species and some of the Western Pale Morning and Pale Evening Duns. In some ways it is similar to the March Brown, but in lighter colors for the tail, body and hackle. The natural mayfly, *Stenonema canadensis*, usually emerges in late afternoon or evening when this fly is particularly effective. Dan Cahill, an avid fisherman and brakeman on the Erie Railroad out of Port Jervis, NY, originated it. At the time (late 1800s) this was an area of great trout water. He fished often with the writer Edward Ringwood Hewitt, developer of the Neversink Skater.

Tied by Chuck Edghill.

Materials Needed

Hook – Standard dry fly hook in sizes 10 through 20
Thread – Tan, yellow or cream
Tail – Light ginger hackle fibers
Body – Light belly fox fur or other cream dubbing
Wings – Wood duck flank fibers, tied upright and divided
Hackle – Light ginger

Tying sequence:

1. Tie in the thread on the hook shank about 1/3rd back from the hook eye.
2. Tie in the wood duck wings facing forward, then use wraps of thread to raise the wings to an upright position. Divide them with thread.
3. Wrap the thread towards the bend of the hook and tie in the tail fibers.
4. Return the thread to the midpoint of the hook shank and tie in the dubbing material, or secure the dubbing to the waxed tying thread.
5. Wrap the tying thread forward to just in back of the wings. (Only if the dubbing is separate from the tying thread.)

6. Wrap the dubbing material up and down the hook shank to form a tapered body, then tie off with the tying thread. Clip or remove any excess dubbing material.
7. Tie in the hackle with the tying thread and clip any excess hackle.
8. Wind the hackle around the hook shank in front of and in back of the wings. Tie off with the tying thread after winding several turns of thread through the hackle to reinforce it. Clip the excess hackle.
9. Make sure that the hackle and wings are out of the way, and finish a small head. Tie off with a whip finish.
10. Seal with head cement.

NO-HACKLE
PALE MORNING DUN

A dry fly that floats in the surface film, rather than on it and thus is an ideal imitation for the early dun stages of mayflies.

Tied by Chuck Edghill.

This is a variation of the standard hackled form of the same fly, but tied without a hackle which allows it to float lower in the water. Many anglers like this style of fly, since it more closely resembles the float of the natural mayfly right after it shucks its nymphal case.

These flies are a lot quicker to tie than traditional hackled styles, but they still require care in the proper placement of the wings. There are many ways to tie this pattern, one of which is described below. An alternative way with an angled wing is to tie in the tail and then the body, adding the angled quill wings as the final step, then adding a small amount of dubbing in front of the wings before tying off.

Materials Needed

Hook – Standard dry fly hook in sizes 12 through 18
Thread – Beige , cream or brown
Tail – White or ginger hackle fibers, split
Body – Grayish cream fur dubbing or synthetic dubbing.
Wings – Matched gray primary or secondary goose quill feathers

Tying sequence:

1. Tie in the thread at midpoint on the hook shank, then wrap tightly to the bend of the hook. Clip any excess thread.
2. Prepare and tie in a small dubbing ball at the bend of the hook prior to tying in the tail to help divide the tail fibers.
3. Tie in the tail of hackle fibers, making sure that they are divided evenly on either side of the dubbing ball.
4. Tie in the body material, or add the dubbing to the waxed tying thread.
5. Wrap the dubbed body forward, or wrap the thread forward to a point about 1/3rd back from the hook eye. Remove any dubbing if using dubbing fixed to the tying thread.

6. Tie in the matched wing quills, facing forward, then raise the wings to an upright position.
7. If using synthetic body material, wrap forward, bringing one final wrap in front of the upright wings, and tie off with the tying thread. If using dubbing, add a small amount of dubbing to the waxed thread and wrap in front of the wings as above.
8. Remove any excess dubbing, make a neat head and tie off with a whip finish. Clip any excess tying thread.
9. Seal with head cement.

IRRESISTIBLE

A beautiful high-floating dry fly showing the original stacked deer hair body as originated by Joe Messinger, Sr.

This fly, originated by Joe Messinger with the tradition continued by his son Joe Messinger, Jr. is a classic trout fly. It was originated in late 1930s, using a spun and stacked deer hair body to create the classic light underbody and dark overbody. Though Joe Jr. ties using methods completely different from standard fly-tying procedures, it can be tied using methods previously described. It has a large profile and with the hollow deer hair is perfect for fishing rough and broken runs, riffles and pocket water. Most commercial patterns show this as a fly with only a spun body of one color, making a simplified version of the original design. In either case, because the body is of clipped deer hair, and because wings and hackle are also tied on, the tying sequence is interrupted to trim the deer hair body before tying on the wings and hackle. This is a brown version, but Joe Sr. also tied the fly in a tan and gray version.

Tied by Joe Messinger, Jr.

Materials Needed

Hook – Standard dry fly hook in sizes 8 through 16
Thread – Black
Tail – Natural deer body hair
Body – Natural brown deer hair stacked over white deer hair, stacked and trimmed to a small tapered body.
Wings - Tan or brown natural deer hair
Hackle – Natural brown deer hair.

Tying sequence:

1. Tie in the thread at the bend of the hook, clip the excess thread, then tie in the tail.
2. Keep the thread in the same position and tie in a tiny bundle of prepared (combed and stacked) deer hair. To do this, hold the dark deer hair bundle at an angle as you bring the thread up, then down on the backside of the hook to retain the deer hair on top of the hook. Hold another bundle of white deer hair on the underside of the hook and repeat the above, to secure the dark deer hair on top and the white deer hair on the bottom. Continue with additional bundles this way to a point about 1/3rd of shank in back of the hook eye.
3. Tie in two half hitches to secure the ties, then use scissors to carefully trim the body to a small tapered bullet shape. Take care to NOT cut the tying thread at this point.
4. After trimming the body to show the stacked white belly and dark back, continue wrapping to add wings of deer hair, tying them forward initially.
5. Build up thread in front of the wings to raise them, then use "wraps" between the two sides of the wing to divide them.
6. Tie in a hackle in back of the wings, and clip the excess.
7. Wind the hackle in front of and in back of the wings, and tie off, then clip the excess hackle.
8. Make a neat head and complete with a whip finish, then clip any excess thread.
9. Seal the head with head cement.

QUILL GORDON

A classic early dry fly originated by Theodore Gordon and tied with a quill body to imitate the segmented body of the natural.

This fly is named for its originator, Theodore Gordon, considered the father of dry-fly fishing in America. This pattern was the first to use stripped peacock quill as a body material to closely imitate the segmented body of mayflies. Other flies, such as the Ginger Quill and Art Flick's Red Quill, use the stripped body design, using hackle quills in place of the peacock quill used on this pattern. The Quill Gordon is a fragile fly, and the body should be coated with head cement after tying the body and before tying the wings and hackle, or carefully coated (avoid the hackle and wings) after the fly is complete. It is one of a number of classic, upright-wing, sparsely and exquisitely tied flies of the Catskill school of fly-tying. It is best fished on quiet pools and is considered a general mayfly pattern. It can also be tied with a gold wire ribbing (optional) to help protect the fragile quill body.

Tied by Chuck Edghill.

Hook – Standard dry fly hook, sizes 12 to 16
Thread – Black or gray
Tail – Dark blue dun hackle fibers
Body – Peacock quill, stripped
Wings – Wood duck flank feathers
Hackle – Dark blue dun

Tying sequence:

1. Tie in the working thread about 1/3rd back from the hook eye, and clip any excess thread.
2. Tie in the wings, facing forward, then use thread in front of the wings and between them to make them upright and divided.
3. Wrap the thread to the bend of the hook, then tie in the tail.
4. Prepare the body material of peacock quill by stripping the fuzz from the quill. Do this by rubbing the herl with a pencil eraser or use bleach, as per the "methods" instructions. Once the quill is prepared, tie down and wrap the thread evenly and tightly forward to the wings.

5. Evenly wrap the peacock quill forward to the wings, and tie off. Clip any excess quill.
6. Tie in the hackle and clip the butt sections.
7. Wind the hackle in back of and in front of the wings, and tie off with the working thread. Clip any excess hackle.
8. Make a neat head in front of the hackle, complete with a whip finish and clip any excess thread.
9. Seal the head with head cement and coat the quill body with head cement for protection.

BROWN BIVISIBLE

Designed for high visibility by both the trout and the angler, this fly floats well in rough water.

The Brown Bivisible fly, in basic brown or other colors as desired, is a simple fly consisting of a tail and hackle. The name Bivisible refers to the two colors of the hackle, presumably one visible to the trout and the other visible to the angler. With the full hackle body, it rides well in rough water where flies are also more difficult to follow and see. While brown is the basic and original color, other colors of hackle can be used in place of brown, or the front hackle of white can be changed to yellow, chartreuse or other colors that may be more easily seen. This is another pattern developed by Edward Ringwood Hewitt, who also developed the Neversink Skater, also called the skating spider. One tip to tying it is to use the brown rear hackle in a slightly smaller size than the front white hackle, so that the profile of the fly will be like a cone, tapered from front to rear.

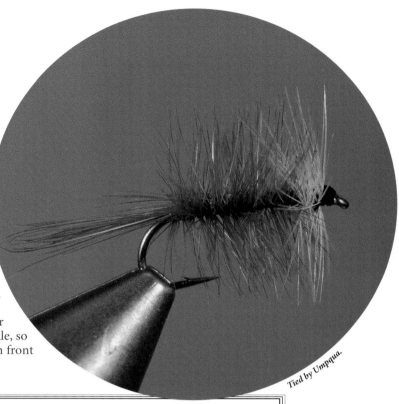

Tied by Umpqua.

Materials Needed

Hook – Standard dry fly hook in sizes 10 through 16
Thread – Brown or black
Tail – Brown hackle fibers
Hackle, rear – Brown hackle, covering about 2/3rds of the hook shank
Hackle, forward – White or cream hackle, tied in front of the brown hackle.

Tying sequence:

1. Tie in the thread at the bend of the hook, then clip the excess thread.
2. Tie in the tail.
3. Tie in several brown hackles and clip the butt ends.
4. Wrap the thread forward to a point about 1/3rd of the shank in back of the hook eye.
5. Wind, or palmer, the brown hackle forward to the thread, then tie off and clip the excess hackle. Since several hackles are usually used, you have the choice of tying several at once or tying each in turn, tying it off with the thread while tying on the next to continue the palmered hackle.
6. Tie in a white or cream hackle, and trim the butt end. Wrap the thread forward to just in back of the hook eye.
7. Wind the hackle forward to the tying thread, and tie off, then clip the excess hackle.
8. Make a neat head, then complete with a whip finish. Clip the excess thread.
9. Seal with head cement.

HENDRICKSON

A classic dry fly that is now tied in a number of variations, including light and dark patterns.

This fly, with its light body and dark hackle/wing has been a standard trout classic since Roy Steenrod developed it in 1916 after a hatch of the naturals on the Beaverkill. It was named in honor of Albert E. Hendrickson, for whom both Steenrod and Theodore Gordon tied flies. Since the original, there have been additions of light and dark Henricksons, and Art Flick came out with a version similar to the original. The following is from the original pattern, as described by Roy Steenrod.

Tied by Chuck Edghill.

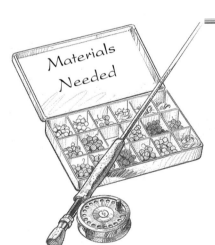

Hook – Standard dry fly hook, sizes 12 to 16
Thread – Yellow or brown
Tail - Crest of golden pheasant
Body – Fawn-colored fur from the belly of a red fox
Wings – Wood duck
Hackle – Dun (blue dun often described)

Tying sequence:

1. Tie in the thread at the midpoint on the hook shank, clip any excess thread and then wrap to a point about 1/3rd back from the hook eye and tie in the wings.
2. Tie in the wings of wood duck facing forward, then raise them with turns of thread in front of the wings. Wrap between the two wing bundles to separate them into a divided wing.
3. Wrap the thread to the bend of the hook.
4. Tie in the tail.
5. Secure the body dubbing to the waxed tying thread, then wrap the body forward to the wings.
6. Remove any excess dubbing and tie in a blue dun hackle, clipping the butt end.
7. Wind the hackle around the hook shank in front of and in back of the wings, then tie off. Clip any excess hackle and bring the thread through the hackle several times for reinforcement.
8. Make a neat head and complete with a whip finish.
9. Seal the head with head cement.

MOSQUITO

A dry fly that will imitate any of the dark and mottled surface flies.

This is an old pattern, and one that can imitate a number of grizzly, gray-mottled mayflies. Or, as the name indicates, it can imitate a mosquito or midge, assuming that the fly is tied small enough or that there are large mosquitoes or midges in your fishing area. With the multi-colored striped body and grizzly wings, it has a life-like buggy look that will take a lot of trout in mid-season.

Tied by Spirit River.

Hook – Standard dry fly hook, size 12 to 20
Thread – Gray
Tail – Grizzly hackle fibers
Body – Stripped grizzly hackle quill
Wings - Grizzly hackle tips, tied divided and upright
Hackle – Grizzly

Tying sequence:

1. Tie in the thread about 1/3rd back on the hook shank, then clip the excess thread.
2. Prepare (strip and clip) the hackle tip wings, then tie them in place facing forward before raising them to an upright divided position with crisscross and forward wraps of thread.
3. Wrap the thread to the bend of the hook, then tie in the tail fibers.
4. Prepare the stripped grizzly hackle quill, tie it in, clip the butt and then wrap the thread forward to the wings.
5. Wrap the quill body forward and tie off just in back of the wings. Clip the excess.
6. Tie in the hackle, then clip the excess butt ends.
7. Wind the hackle around the hook shank, in front of and in back of the wings.
8. Tie off the hackle, and clip the excess.
9. Make a small neat head, complete with a whip finish and clip the excess thread.
10. Seal with head cement.

BLUE-WINGED OLIVE

A classic dry fly that is so commonly used that it is often abbreviated as BWO.

This fly can be used on both Eastern and Western waters. In larger sizes, according to Dave Hughes' book, *TROUT FLIES*, it will imitate some of the smaller green drake mayflies, and in small sizes will imitate some of the little olive (Baetis) species. It is an easy tie of a light-colored pattern that is effective in mid to late spring on most waters. This tie is with hackle tips, but it can also be tied upright and divided with mallard quill sections.

Tied by Pacific Fly Group.

Materials Needed

Hook – Standard dry fly in sizes 14 through 20
Thread – Olive
Tail – Dark dun hackle fibers
Body – Medium olive fur or synthetic dubbing
Wings - Dark olive hackle tips tied upright and divided
Hackle – Dark dun

Tying sequence:

1. Tie in the thread about 1/3rd back on the hook shank, then clip the excess thread.
2. Prepare (strip and clip) the hackle tip wings, then tie them in place facing forward before raising them to an upright divided position with criss-cross and forward wraps of thread.
3. Wrap the thread to the bend of the hook, then tie in the tail fibers.
4. Prepare to tie in the body by adding dubbing to the waxed tying thread or tying in synthetic dubbing material. If doing the latter, wrap the thread forward to the wings, followed by the body material. Tie off and clip excess.
5. If using dubbing, wrap the dubbed thread (body) forward, then remove any excess.
6. Tie in the hackle, then clip the excess butt ends.
7. Wind the hackle around the hook shank, in front of and in back of the wings.
8. Tie off the hackle, and clip the excess.
9. Make a small neat head, complete with a whip finish and clip the excess thread.
10. Seal with head cement.

RED QUILL

This is a classic Art Flick pattern and another must for Eastern trout streams.

The Red Quill is an old Art Flick pattern from his book *ART FLICK'S STREAMSIDE GUIDE*. According to Flick, this fly represents the male of the mayfly. The female is represented by the Hendrickson. Both are effective during Hendrickson hatches on Eastern streams. The name Red Quill really comes from an older English fly, and in this American form is very similar to the Hendrickson, except for the body. Flick tied both this and the Hendrickson in size 12 only, but it can be tied in any size as required.

Tied by Riverborn Fly Company.

Hook – Standard dry fly, size 12 to 16
Thread – Olive
Tail – Dun hackle fibers
Body – Rhode Island Red cock feather, stripped and soaked
Wings – Mandarin or wood duck drake flank feather
Hackle – Natural blue dun

Tying sequence:

1. Tie in the thread about 1/3rd back on the hook shank, then clip the excess thread.
2. Prepare (strip and clip) the hackle tip wings, then tie them in place facing forward before raising them to an upright divided position with crisscross and forward wraps of thread.
3. Wrap the thread to the bend of the hook, then tie in the tail fibers.
4. Prepare to tie in the body by adding dubbing to the waxed tying thread or tying in synthetic dubbing material. If doing the latter, wind the thread forward to the wings, followed by the body material. Tie off and clip excess.
5. If using dubbing, wrap the thread (body) forward, then remove any excess.
6. Tie in the hackle, then clip the excess butt ends.
7. Wind the hackle around the hook shank, in front of and in back of the wings.
8. Tie off the hackle, and clip the excess.
9. Make a small neat head, complete it with a whip finish and clip the excess thread.
10. Seal with head cement.

GRAY FOX

Another easy-to-tie and very effective pattern for dry fly fishing.

This is a Preston Jennings pattern, also listed in Art Flick's book on trout flies and a popular one with most Eastern and Western trout fishermen. It often appears when the March Brown mayflies are also on the water, and most streams have both insects. Flick noted that the trout seem to prefer this fly after the March Brown hatch is over. He preferred the March Brown for fishing right before and during the hatch, reserving the Gray Fox for late in the hatch or after the March Brown hatch ended.

Tied by Chuck Edghill.

Hook – Standard dry fly hook, size 12 through 16
Thread – Yellow or primrose
Tail – Ginger hackle fibers
Body – Light fawn-colored fur from red fox, or synthetic equivalent
Wings – Mallard drake flank feather
Hackle – Mixed golden ginger and grizzly

Tying sequence:

1. Tie in the thread about 1/3rd back on the hook shank, then clip the excess thread.
2. Prepare (strip and clip) the hackle tip wings, then tie them in place facing forward before raising them to an upright divided position with crisscross and forward wraps of thread.
3. Wrap the thread to the bend of the hook, then tie in the tail fibers.
4. Prepare to tie in the body by adding dubbing to the waxed tying thread or tying in synthetic dubbing material. If doing the later, wrap the thread forward to the wings, followed by the body material. Tie off and clip excess.
5. If using dubbing, wrap the thread (body) forward, then remove any excess.
6. Tie in the hackle, then clip the excess butt ends.
7. Wind the hackle around the hook shank, in front of and in back of the wings.
8. Tie off the hackle, and clip the excess.
9. Make a small head, and complete the fly with a whip finish, then clip the excess thread.
10. Seal with head cement.

GINGER QUILL

This pattern uses a quill body, as does the Quill Gordon, but is in a much lighter shade.

The Ginger Quill is another of several popular mayfly patterns with a stripped quill body that closely resembles the dark and light segments of many mayflies. It is traditionally tied with a quill wing segment from mallard, tied upright and divided. As with most flies tied like this, it is best fished in pools over feeding trout that are actively taking mayflies in this same color and design. It is basically an Eastern pattern.

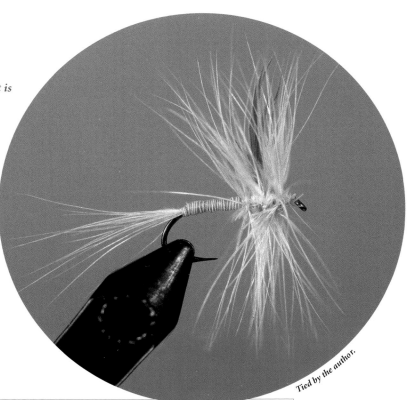

Tied by the author.

Hook – Standard dry fly hook, sizes 12 to 18
Thread – Cream or light yellow
Tail – Ginger or dark cream hackle fibers
Body – Stripped ginger quill or peacock quill
Wings – Mallard quill sections, tied in upright and divided
Hackle - Ginger

Tying sequence:

1. Tie in the thread about 1/3rd back on the hook shank, then clip the excess thread.
2. Prepare (strip and clip) the hackle tip wings, then tie them in place facing forward before raising them to an upright divided position with criss-cross and forward wraps of thread.
3. Wrap the thread to the bend of the hook, then tie in the tail fibers.
4. Prepare to tie in the body by adding dubbing to the waxed tying thread or tying in synthetic dubbing material. If doing the latter, wrap the thread forward to the wings, followed by the body material. Tie off and clip excess.
5. If using dubbing, wrap the thread (body) forward, then remove any excess.
6. Tie in the hackle, then clip the excess butt ends.
7. Wind the hackle around the hook shank, in front of and in back of the wings.
8. Tie off the hackle, and clip the excess.
9. Make a small neat head, and finish the fly with a whip finish.
10. Clip the excess thread and seal with head cement.

BLACK GNAT

This basic black pattern is tied in both this dry fly style as well as a wet fly.

The Black Gnat is a dark mayfly imitation that can serve as a substitute for a Dark Hendrickson or Dark Cahill. It is often good to fish a fly that will stand out a little from other dark naturals on the water, particularly during early morning or late evening fishing. Also, as a dark fly, it is often more visible to the angler than are lighter tan, cream, brown or gray flies.

Tied by Spirit River.

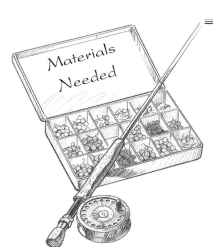

Materials Needed

Hook – Standard dry fly, sizes 12 through 18
Thread – Black
Tail – Black hackle fibers
Body – Black dubbing fur or black synthetic body material
Wings – Upright and divided wing of mallard quill sections
Hackle – Black

Tying sequence:

1. Tie in the thread about 1/3rd back on the hook shank, then clip the excess thread.
2. Prepare the wing quill segments, then tie them in place facing forward before raising them to an upright divided position with criss-cross and forward wraps of thread.
3. Wrap the thread to the bend of the hook, then tie in the tail fibers.
4. Prepare to tie in the body by adding dubbing to the waxed tying thread or tying in synthetic dubbing material. If doing the latter, wind the thread forward to the wings, followed by the body material. Tie off and clip any excess.
5. If using dubbing, wrap the thread (body) forward, then remove any excess.
6. Tie in the hackle, then clip the excess butt ends.
7. Wind the hackle around the hook shank, in front of and in back of the wings.
8. Tie off the hackle, and clip the excess.
9. Make a head to the fly, then complete with a whip finish and clip the excess thread.
10. Seal with head cement.

GREEN DRAKE THORAX

Green drakes are popular mayfly imitations. The thorax pattern is a departure from the more classic standard dry fly style.

Tied by Umpqua.

Thorax ties are a little different from other ties, in that they are tied with the wing slightly farther back than on traditional dry flies. Also, the hackle is clipped on the bottom to make the fly float on or in the surface film, rather than above it, as with the tail and hackle tip support of standard Catskill-style dries. This more closely imitates the dun stage of the insect – right after the insect has emerged from the nymphal form and before the wings have become dry and transparent as with the spinner forms. As with the traditional dries, they are best fished on flat, calm pools and runs, and were developed for this fishing by Vince Marinaro, who wrote about them in his book *A MODERN DRY FLY CODE.*

Materials Needed

Hook – Standard dry fly hook, sizes 10 through 14
Tail – Cream or brown hackle fibers, split or splayed to support the fly
Body – Cream or yellow yarn or dubbing - optional, rib with thin brown yarn
Wings – Yellow or tan turkey flat feather
Hackle – Bronze dun and grizzly mixed

Tying sequence:

1. Tie in the thread about 1/3rd the shank length in back of the hook eye. Clip the excess thread.
2. Prepare (clip a small bundle) of turkey flat fibers and tie them in at this point, the tips facing forward. Clip the excess butt material. Raise the wings to an upright position.
3. Wrap the thread to the bend of the hook, then tie in the tail fibers.
4. Split with figure- eight wraps of thread or splay the tail fibers to make them better support the fly. Another possibility is to add a small ball of dubbing (the same dubbing used for the body) to the hook shank, and then tie in the tail fibers. The small dubbing ball will cause the tail fibers to split into a forked tail.
5. Add dubbing to the waxed working thread, or tie in a length of synthetic dubbing body material.
6. Wrap the thread (and dubbing) forward and continue around the base of the wings to finish off ahead of the wings and just in back of the hook eye. Alternately, wrap the thread forward to the wings, then wrap the body dubbing material forward, around the wings and to the hook eye and back to be tied off. Clip the excess.
7. Tie in a prepared hackle and clip the excess butt material.
8. Wrap a full hackle around the hook shank both in front of and in back of the upright wings. Tie off and clip the excess hackle.
9. Make a small neat head, complete with a whip finish and clip the excess thread.
10. Seal with head cement.

LOOPWING DUN

Loop wings are another way to imitate the opaque or translucent wings of a dun or emerging mayfly. Loop wings can be tied in any color, with this a typical pattern.

Loopwings are another way to form wings on a dry fly as fly-tyers try to closely suggest or imitate the silhouette and shape of an emergent mayfly in the dun stage. The spinner stage of a mayfly has dry, transparent wings and usually a lighter colored body. For those, light colors and fine tufts of synthetic poly for wing material are used. Loopwings are generally used to imitate the dun mayfly. Upright loopwings are another way to form wings that are the principle part of a fly that a trout sees first through its window in the surface film of water.

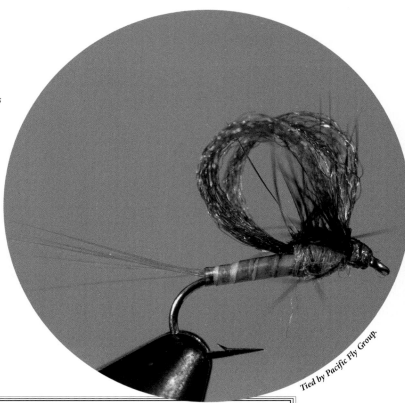

Tied by Pacific Fly Group.

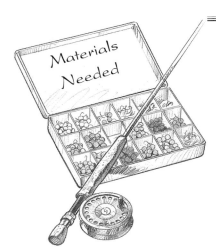

Materials Needed

Hook – Standard dry fly hook, sizes 12 to 16
Thread – Gray
Tail – Gray squirrel tail or gray hackle fibers
Body – Gray fur dubbing, gray synthetic dubbing material, or tan floss
Wings – Mallard or teal flank fibers, long enough to make a loop over the hook shank and form wings
Hackle – Gray or grizzly

Tying sequence:

1. Tie in the thread at about 1/3rd back from the hook eye. Clip the excess thread.

2. Prepare loop wing fibers by using a few long hackle fibers, and tie them down near their hackle tips. (Ted Leeson and Jim Schollmeyer in their excellent book *THE FLY TIER'S BENCHSIDE REFERENCE* recommend four to six fibers.)

3. Use a bodkin, held above the hook and at right angles to fold over the hackle fibers. The height of this fold should be about two times that of the hook gap.

4. Tie down the ends of the loop wings and clip any excess.

5. Wrap the thread to the bend of the hook then tie in the tail fibers.

6. Tie in the body dubbing, or add body dubbing to the waxed tying thread. Alternatively, use floss.

7. Wrap the thread forward, followed by the body material, or wrap the dubbing and remove any excess at the loop wings.

8. Tie in a hackle, and wind it around the hook shank in front of and in back of the loop wing.

9. Clip the excess hackle, then wrap a neat head and complete the fly with a whip finish. Clip the excess thread.

10. Seal with head cement.

CAENIS SPINNER

Caenis imitations are always tiny flies that, along with Tricos (Tricorythodes) and Baetis, are among the smallest that trout fishermen will fish. This pattern is photographed at a slight angle to show the spent poly wings.

The Caenis mayflies are tiny, about the size of the more widely known and popular Tricos (tricorithides) and are most common in lakes and slower moving stretches of trout streams. They can come out in huge numbers and produce excellent hatches for lake fishing and some stream fishing. As with the Tricos, they can make for challenging fishing due to the small size of the fly used and the necessary fine tippet required on the leader.

Tied by the author.

Materials Needed

Hook – Standard dry fly in sizes 18 to 24
Thread – Black
Tail – Light dun hackle fibers
Body – White thread
Wings – Clear or white synthetic poly fibers

Tying sequence:

1. Tie in the thread at the bend of the hook, clip the excess thread, then tie in the tail fibers.
2. Clip the excess tail fibers, then tie in white thread for a body material.
3. Wind the black thread forward, followed by the white thread wrapped for a body. Clip the excess white thread.
4. Figure-8 a small bundle of poly material as a wing. Make sure that the poly wing is flat – right angles to the plane of the hook, and at right angles to the hook shank. Trim the wing to length on each side, if required.
5. Wrap the thread forward and make a neat head, completed with a whip finish.
6. Clip the excess thread, then seal with head cement.

BROWN DRAKE SPINNER

Brown drakes are another of the larger mayflies. Most spent-wing patterns are tied with poly wings. This one has a support of deer hair under the poly wings to aid in flotation.

This fly imitates the spinner or imago form of the brown drake, although it can be tied in different colors to imitate local green drakes as well. As a spinner fly, it has the poly wing material tied flat — or spent — to suggest the wings of the dead or exhausted insect that are flat on the water. Ideally, these wings should be tied sparsely to suggest the transparent wings of the natural. This lack of hackle also helps this fly to ride in the surface film, rather than above it as with a Catskill dun pattern and thus presents a more natural appearance of the imitation. Brown drakes are found throughout the East and West to the Rockies.

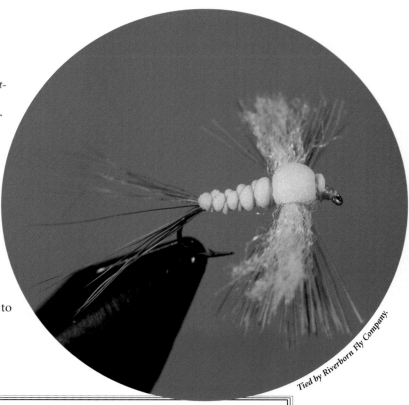

Tied by Riverborn Fly Company.

Hook – Standard dry fly hook, sizes 10 to 14
Thread – Tan or cream
Tail – Cream or light brown hackle fibers, somewhat splayed
Body – Yellow, or dark yellow dubbing or foam body material
Ribbing – Brown thread or gold oval tinsel
Wing - White or light-colored poly material or fibers (optional: deer hair for added floatation, as with this fly)

Tying sequence:

1. Tie in the thread about 1/4 to 1/3rd back from the hook eye.
2. Tie in a sparse bundle of the poly material for the wings, using crisscross and Figure-8s to secure it. Tie this wing at right angles to the hook plane and horizontal.
3. Wrap the thread to the bend of the hook, then tie in the tail fibers.
4. Tie in the ribbing, or use thread as ribbing.
5. Tie in the body material, or add dubbing to the waxed tying thread. Tie down foam.
6. Wrap the thread forward to the wings, followed by the body material, which is then tied off, or wrap the

dubbing to this point. If using foam, wrap the thread back and forth over the foam body.
7. Follow with the ribbing spiral wrapped around the body, then tie off the spiral wrap with the thread. Clip the excess tinsel or thread ribbing.
8. Add more dubbing, if required, then wrap the dubbing or the thread forward to the hook eye. If using body material, follow with a body wrap, then tie off. If using dubbing, remove any excess dubbing.
9. Make a neat head, tie off with a whip finish and clip any excess thread.
10. Seal with head cement.

EXTENDED-BODY MAYFLY, GREEN DRAKE

Of the many ways to tie extended bodies for mayflies, this is perhaps the easiest and is also very life-like.

Extended-body Mayflies are an attempt to tie flies that closely imitate the delicate, arched body and tail of the natural form of the insect. Initially, some extended-body methods involved complex tying of materials on curved pieces of monofilament, which were then tied to the hook with the remainder of the body material wrapped around the hook shank to complete the fly. Today, these and many other methods are still possible, although they often make flies that are a little stiffer and thicker than the actual insect they are trying to imitate, while at the same time being more difficult to tie. One easy solution is to tie flies using moose mane for the tails and green yarn for the extended body. Here is how to make a simple Extended-body Mayfly using these materials.

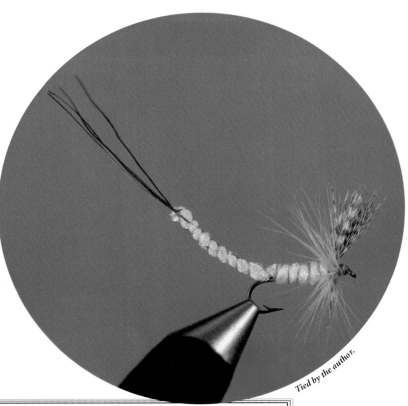

Tied by the author.

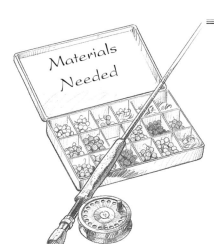

Hook – Standard dry fly hook, sizes 6 through 12
Thread –Tan or green
Tail - Moose mane
Body – Light green yarn
Wings – Mallard flank or body fibers, tied upright
Hackle – Blue dun or light ginger

Tying sequence:

1. Hold two to four fibers of moose mane with two strands of light green yarn between the thumb and index fingers of both hands
2. Grip the thread with the right hand and turn the bobbin two turns over the thread and around the yarn and moose mane.
3. Once the thread is captured by the turns of thread, allow the bobbin to hang free. Turn the yarn and moose mane towards you. Continue this to lock the thread in place and then spiral wrap the thread along the yarn body by turning the yarn as the thread spirals.
4. If necessary, pull on the moose mane to adjust the length of the tail appropriate to the body length and fly size.
5. Once the length of the extended body has been achieved, hold the body on the hook shank and continue to wrap the thread over the yarn body and the hook shank. Clip the excess yarn and moose mane.

6. Wrap the thread forward and tie in the wings, tips forward.
7. Wrap in front of the wings to raise them to an upright position.
8. Wind the thread back to the tie down point of the body and tie in a length of light green yarn.
9. Wrap the yarn forward to the wings, then hold the yarn in place while you follow with a spiral ribbing of thread.
10. Tie off the yarn with the thread.
11. Tie in the butt end of the hackle and then wrap the hackle around the hook shank in front of and in back of the wings.
12. Tie off the hackle and clip any excess.
13. Wind the thread forward of the hackle, make a neat head and tie off with a whip finish.
14. Seal the head with head cement.

HAYSTACK

The Haystack, unlike the similar Comparadun, has deer hair for the tail as well as the wing. It floats low to imitate dun mayflies.

Tied by the author.

The Haystack is thought to be the precursor of the Comparadun flies that have the same principle of no hackle, but a flared wing of deer or elk hair that helps to float the fly in the surface film. The Haystack was the development of Fran Betters, who fished it on Catskill and Adirondack streams in the 1950s and later. The main difference between this and the Comparadun series is the flared tail of the Comparadun flies that helps them to float better and to stay upright more often.

Materials Needed

Hook – Standard dry fly hook, sizes 10 through 16
Thread – Tan or brown
Tail – Tan or brown deer or elk hair
Body – Tan or brown dubbing fur or synthetic dubbing body material
Wings - Tan or brown deer or elk hair, flared to the sides

Tying sequence:

1. Tie in the thread about 1/3rd back from the hook eye, and clip the excess thread.
2. Prepare (clip, comb and stack) deer or elk hair, and tie in at the thread point, with the tips of the hair pointing forward.
3. Wind the thread through the wing hair to raise it to a vertical position. To make this easy, run it through a small bundle of the hair, repeating with successive bundles to raise the entire bundle to an upright position.
4. Clip any excess butt material and wrap the thread to the bend of the hook.
5. Tie in a small bundle of deer or elk hair, for the tails then tie in the body material or add dubbing to the waxed tying thread.
6. Wrap the dubbing forward or alternatively, wrap the thread forward followed by the body dubbing. Wrap around the base of the wing and wrap to just in back of the hook eye. Tie off or remove the excess dubbing.
7. Make a neat head, then complete the fly with a whip finish and clip the excess thread.
8. Seal with head cement.

STIMULATOR

Many Western patterns for trout imitate salmon flies in both nymphal and adult stages. This popular pattern is a combination imitative and attractor pattern.

This is a Randall Kaufmann design that is a great Western multi-purpose fly. In large sizes you can use this like a Muddler or as a grasshopper imitation. In these sizes you could also fish it sub-surface as a minnow or sculpin imitation, although it is designed and almost always fished as a dry. In medium sizes it can imitate the Western salmon fly or golden stone fly, and in small sizes will work as a pattern for little yellow stoneflies. This is really a variation of the Improved Sofa Pillow, which has an orange body. The Improved Sofa Pillow is a palmered-body variation of the original Sofa Pillow. Variations include different colors of abdomen, thorax and hackle.

Tied by McKenzie.

Materials Needed

Hook – Standard 2X to 4X long streamer hook in sizes 4 through 14
Thread – Orange
Tail – Deer or elk body hair
Body, abdomen – Yellow fur dubbing or synthetic body material
Body, thorax – Orange fur dubbing or synthetic body material
Ribbing – Grizzly hackle, palmered
Wings - Deer or elk body hair
Hackle – Grizzly

Tying sequence:

1. Tie in the thread at the bend of the hook. Clip the excess thread.
2. Tie in the tail of deer or elk body hair.
3. Tie in the tip end of the palmering grizzly hackle, then the yellow body material. (This is easier than dubbing, although that is also a possibility.)
4. Wrap the thread forward to a position about 1/3rd of the shank in back of the hook eye, then wrap the body material forward and tie off. Clip the excess body material.
5. Palmer wrap the hackle forward to the thread and tie off. Clip any excess hackle.
6. Tie in the orange thorax material, then tie down a bundle of deer or elk hair as a down wing after first clipping, combing and stacking it.
7. Clip the excess butts of the wing, then tie in a grizzly hackle feather.
8. Wrap the thread forward to the hook eye, then follow with the orange body material. Tie off the body material and clip the excess.
9. Wind the hackle around the hook shank, then tie it off after slightly palmering it forward to the thread position. Clip the excess, make a neat head and complete with a whip finish.
10. Clip the thread and seal with head cement.

RENEGADE

There are several patterns that use fore and aft hackle turns to aid in flotation. This is a popular one, particularly for Western waters.

The Renegade is a Western fly that can be fished dry on the rough Western streams or fished as a wet fly with the hackle tied in a flared back position. It is a classic Western fore-and-aft hackle pattern. This is a style that goes back a number of years, with the thought that the two hackles – one each in front of and in back of the body – will help to float the fly. The two colors also achieve the same effect as the Bivisible, in that the colors presumably make it easier for both the trout and the angler to see. Tie it with flared back soft hackle to use as a wet fly.

Tied by Riverborn Fly Company.

Materials Needed

Hook – Standard dry fly hook, sizes 10 through 16
Thread – Black
Tag – Flat gold tinsel
Rear Hackle – Brown
Body – Peacock herl
Front Hackle – White

Tying sequence:

1. Tie in the thread at the midpoint on the hook shank, clip the excess and wind the thread to the bend of the hook.

2. Tie in the flat tinsel for the tag, and make a few even wraps of the thread forward.

3. Wrap the tinsel evenly to the thread and tie off.

4. Tie in the peacock herl, the herl facing forward.

5. Tie in a brown hackle, clip the butt end and wind it around the hook shank at the rear of the fly.

6. Tie off the hackle, clip the excess and wind thread through the hackle to strengthen it.

7. Wrap the thread forward to in back of the hook eye.

8. Wrap the peacock herl forward and tie off with the thread. Clip the excess. (An alternative is to tie in and wind the hackle, then tie in the peacock herl, wrap the thread forward, followed by the peacock herl.)

9. Tie in a white hackle, clip the butt end and wind it around the hook shank.

10. Tie off and clip the excess hackle.

11. Make a neat head, then tie off the fly with a whip finish. Clip the excess thread

12. Seal with head cement.

DANCING CADDIS

The innovative tier Gary LaFontaine has developed a lot of unusual patterns over the years, with this one of his most popular caddis patterns.

This is a Gary LaFontaine pattern from his book, *CADDISFLIES*. It is one of many that this innovative writer has developed over the years, and unusual in that it is tied "upside down" so that the hook rides point up. It is similar in design to the commercially tied Water Wisp flies that are tied both upside down and reversed, with the tail at the eye of the hook.

Tied by Chuck Edghill.

Hook – Standard dry fly hook, sizes 10 to 18
Thread – Olive
Body – Pale olive dubbing
Wings - Natural elk or deer body hair
Hackle – Blue dun, trimmed on the bottom (note that the fly rides hook point up)

Tying sequence:

1. Place the hook in the vise with the point up but held by the hook bend.
2. Tie in the working thread at a point about 1/3rd back from the hook eye. Clip any excess thread.
3. Add a thin layer of dubbing to the waxed tying thread, and wrap the dubbing down the hook shank to the bend and back up to the tie-down point. Remove any excess dubbing.
4. Clip, comb and stack a wing of deer hair, hold over the body and tie in place. This wing should be no longer than the hook shank. Clip any excess hair in front of the tie-down point.
5. Tie in the hackle, and wind around the hook shank at the tie-down point, gradually working forward to fill in the hook shank area.
6. Tie off with the thread and clip any excess hackle.
7. Make a neat head and complete with a whip finish. Clip any excess thread.
8. Seal the head with head cement, then trim the bottom hackle fibers flat with scissors.

HUMPY

The desire to create dry flies that float high and long has led to this pattern with the body of tied deer hair in addition to the tail and wing.

For a trout, a Humpy must look like a sizable piece of meat when compared to the delicate dries or the natural mayflies that are the cause of much surface activity by trout and angler alike. It often floats in or on the surface film rather than rising high on hackle tips as do most dry flies. And with the body of hollow deer hair, it will ride through the roughest water and still stay on top – or bounce back up if it gets dunked. It is not imitative of any specific insect, but one of those buggy flies that are great, particularly when fishing through rough water or when fishing pocket water or riffles. While the basic fly is brown, you can tie it in any color you wish using dyed deer hair. It does take a little practice to get the right size deer hair bundle for the size hook you are using, but it is worth the effort in the tying result and fishing success on any water. This is a originally a Western tie, and author Terry Hellekson (*FISH FLIES*) describes it as a more popular variation of the very similar Horner's Deer Hair, originated by Jack Horner of San Francisco.

Tied by Chuck Edghill.

Hook – Standard dry fly hook in sizes 8 through 16
Thread – Yellow or tan
Tail – Moose body hair
Body – Tying thread as a base on the hook, over which deer hair is arched.
Wings – Deer body hair
Hackle – Brown or brown and grizzly

Tying sequence:

1. Tie in the thread at midpoint on the hook, then wrap to the bend of the hook and tie in the tail.
2. Wrap the thread forward over the excess tail material to a point about 1/3rd back from the hook eye. Tie in the body/wing material of deer hair with the tips facing to the rear. This bundle, clipped from the skin, underhair removed and stacked, should be about three times the shank length, since it will be wrapped to the rear, then folded over to form the hump of the Humpy, and finally raised to an upright position for the wings.
3. (An alternative to the above is to tie in a bundle at the tail that is about 2-1/4 times the length of the hook shank, work the thread forward and then fold over the tie.)
4. Wrap the thread to the rear over the deer hair, and then back forward to the 1/3rd position in back of the hook eye.
5. Separate the deer hair from the moose hair tail, and fold the deer hair over the hook. Tie down with the working thread.
6. Bring the tying thread in front of the deer hair tips as you raise them, and make several wraps of the thread to keep the wings raised to an upright position.
7. Use the working thread to divide the deer hair tips into two equal parts, separating them with "X's" of thread between the two bundles.
8. Bring the thread to just in back of the wings and tie in the hackles. Two hackles are best, both brown or brown and grizzly. Clip the butt ends of the hackles.
9. Bring the thread forward to just in back of the hook eye.
10. Wind the hackles individually around the hook shank in back of and in front of the wings, and tie off. Clip any excess hackle.
11. Pull back the hackle and wings to make room to tie in a neat head, then complete with a whip finish.
12. Seal the head with head cement.

DUN VARIANT

Variants are dry flies that have longer tails and larger hackles than would normally be used. Thus, they float high and skate on the water nicely.

This is an Art Flick pattern, one designed to replace the Red Quill that he sometimes used to take trout hitting gray-bodied mayflies. He liked the variant in that it rode high and perhaps best imitated the light touch of mayflies on the waters surface. Basically, variants are a style of tying as opposed to a particular pattern. As such, they consist of longer than normal tails and larger than normal hackles. They are sort of oversized dries tied with a normal body and hook. Just how big the tail and hackle should be is somewhat subjective, although most tyers consider that they should be about two to three fly sizes larger. Thus, for a size 16 variant, you should use a hackle and tail sized for a size 12 fly. Although popularized by Art Flick, this is basically a style of tying developed by an English angler. This a Dun Variant, but variants can be tied based on any of the classic dry fly patterns, particularly those of the Catskill style, although usually they are tied without wings.

Tied by Chuck Edghill.

Hook – Standard dry fly hook, sizes 12 to 18
Thread – Gray
Tail – Medium blue dun hackle fibers
Body – Stripped hackle quill from the neck of a Rhode Island Red cock.
Hackle – Medium to dark blue dun

Tying sequence:

1. Tie in the thread at the midpoint on the hook shank, clip the excess thread and then wrap tightly to the bend of the hook.
2. Tie in the tail.
3. Tie in a well-soaked stripped hackle quill and wrap the thread forward to a point about 1/3rd in back of the hook eye. (The quill will have to be well soaked to be flexible and wrap without splitting on the thin diameter hook shank.)
4. Wrap the hackle quill evenly and tightly around the hook shank, and tie off at the thread position.
5. Tie in the hackle and trim the butt end.
6. Wind the hackle around the hook shank and then tie off, clipping the end of the hackle feather.
7. Make a neat head in front of the hackle, then tie off with a whip finish.
8. Seal the head with head cement.

PALE MORNING DUN

Unlike the previous No-Hackle Pale Morning Dun, this is tied in standard dry fly style.

The PMD, as it is sometimes called, is a very light colored basic mayfly imitation that can be tied in a number of ways. Even with one basic quill wing version (of which this is one pattern) there are variations as to body (hackle stem quills or fur or synthetic dubbing) and even to thorax ties and parachute ties. This just points out that there are often many variations and subtle changes of all patterns along with ways in which to tie them. This is just one of many examples of that fact.

Tied by Riverborn Fly Company.

Hook – Standard dry fly hook, sizes 14 through 18
Thread – Very light yellow
Tail – Pale blue dun hackle fibers
Body – Light, pale yellow olive dubbing
Wing - Very pale gray duck wing quill sections
Hackle – Pale blue dun

Tying sequence:

1. Tie in the working thread at a point about 1/3rd back from the hook eye.
2. Prepare matching sections of light gray duck quill wing sections and tie in place, facing forward.
3. Use the thread to build up in front of the quills and around them to make an upright wing.
4. Wrap the thread to the bend of the hook, and tie in the tail.
5. Wax the tying thread and add light yellow dubbing, then wrap forward to make a body. Remove any excess dubbing.
6. Tie in a hackle and trim the butt end.
7. Wind the hackle around the hook shank, in back of and in front of the wing.
8. Tie off the hackle, clip the excess and make a neat head.
9. Complete with a whip finish and then clip the excess thread.
10. Seal with head cement.

PARACHUTE ADAMS

Almost any dry fly can be tied in parachute style in which the hackle is parallel to the water to allow for a lower more natural float. This is one example.

Parachute flies are dries, but tied completely differently from standard dry flies. The fly is tied with a vertical post where the wings normally are (and sometimes uses standard wings as the post) then the hackle wound horizontally around the post or wings. In essence the hackle is at right angles to the vertical wrap of wings on traditional ties. This gives the fly more surface area and contact of the hackle with the surface of the water, and also causes the fly to ride differently. Parachute flies ride with their body on or in the surface film, rather than riding on the tail and hackle tips as do traditional dry flies (theoretically, at least). Sometimes materials are changed from the original pattern, either for better visibility (as with the white calf tail wings here) or for improved flotation (as with the moose body hair tail here).

Tied by Chuck Edghill.

Hook – Standard dry fly, sizes 12 through 18
Thread – Black
Tail – Moose body hair
Body – Gray muskrat fur dubbing
Post or Wings – White calf tail
Hackle – Mixed brown and grizzly

Tying sequence:

1. Tie in the thread on the hook shank about 1/3rd back from the hook eye. Clip any excess thread.

2. Tie in the calf tail wings, facing forward, then raise them to a single (not divided) upright position through the positioning of the thread in front of and around the base of the wings.

3. Wrap the thread to the bend of the hook and tie in the tail of moose.

4. Wax the thread and add muskrat dubbing or a suitable grayish synthetic.

5. Wrap the dubbing thread up to the wing post, remove any excess dubbing and make an additional turn or two with the thread.

6. Prepare the hackles, tie them on the hook shank forward of the wing post and clip any butt ends.

7. Wind the hackle around the wing post, holding the post as you do so to prevent it from shifting position or the hackle from sliding up and off. (Some prefer to wrap clockwise around the stem, others prefer to wrap counterclockwise. Either will work. Also, if you tie a lot of parachute flies, a gallows tool will help here to hold up the post while winding the hackle.)

8. After enough turns of hackle (two or three, normally) hold the hackle tip and wrap over it with the tying thread. If you do not wish to wrap over the previously wrapped hackle fibers, hold them out of the way with your left hand and run the thread over the hook shank to bind the hackle tips. Trim any excess hackle tips.

9. Continue to hold the hackle up and out of the way and make a small neat head on the hook shank, them complete with a whip finish.

10. Hold the hackle out of the way and seal the head with head cement.

GRIFFITH'S GNAT

This is a little imitation of many midge and other small naturals. It is easy to tie despite its small size.

George Griffith, one of the founders of Trout Unlimited, developed this simple but effective midge pattern. It is a dry fly and looks the same as a Bivisible, albeit in a different color. It is tied differently, in that it has a palmered hackle over a simple body to give it a look of some substance. It is easy to see on the water, and especially effective in the smallest sizes. It is a standard for any fly box as a generic midge pattern that will work anywhere. If desired, you can tie it in different colors, using different colors of fur or synthetic dubbing, and even different color hackle if desired. It floats in the surface film rather than on it as with a traditional dry fly, and thus closely imitates midges that are often found struggling in the surface film.

Tied by Chuck Edghill.

Hook – Standard dry fly hook in sizes 16 through 22
Thread – Black
Body – Peacock herl
Rib – Fine gold wire (though this is optional)
Hackle – Grizzly, palmered

Tying sequence:

1. Tie in the thread in back of the hook eye, and wrap the thread evenly to the bend of the hook. Clip any excess thread.
2. Tie in the grizzly hackle and trim the butt end.
3. Tie in the peacock herl and wrap the thread to just in back of the hook eye.
4. Wrap the peacock herl forward, and tie off in back of the hook eye, then clip any excess herl.
5. Wrap the hackle forward, palmering the hackle through the peacock, then tie off and clip and excess hackle.
6. Make a small head, and complete with a whip finish, then seal with head cement.

ROYAL WULFF

This white-winged variation of the old standard Royal Coachman is a high-floater and also highly visible. It is one of many Wulff styles.

The Wulff flies, designed by Lee Wulff in 1929 when fishing with Dan Bailey in the Adirondacks, are basically a series of rough-water hair-wing flies that come in a variety of colors and patterns. While the basic design comes from Lee Wulff, some subsequent patterns are from others such as Gary LaFontaine (Were Wulff), Fran Betters (Ausable Wulff), Dan Bailey (Black Wulff). The design has been adapted almost universally, and can be found as a variation in a number of standard patterns. Some, like the Royal Wulff, White Wulff and the Ausable Wulff have white wings for easy angler visibility; others do not. All are heavily hackled flies for high long floats in rough water. They are great Western trout flies.

Tied by Pacific Fly Group.

Materials Needed

Hook – Standard dry fly hook, 1X to 2X long if possible, in sizes 8 through 14
Thread – Black
Tail – Brown bucktail
Body – Bands of peacock herl, red floss, and peacock herl
Wings – White calf tail
Hackle – Dark brown

Tying sequence:

1. Tie in the thread in back of the eye, then clip any excess thread.
2. Prepare a bundle of calf tail for the wings. For this, clip close to the skin, comb out any underfur and try to stack it (even the tips) as much as possible. (Because it is so kinky, this is very difficult with calf tail.)
3. Tie down the bundle of calf tail, facing forward, at a spot about 1/3rd back from the eye of the hook.
4. Divide the bundle into two parts, and separate them with "X" wraps of thread, bringing the thread around each post as well as between the two wings.
5. Wrap the thread to the bend of the hook and tie in the tail.
6. Tie in a strand of peacock herl and wrap the thread forward about 1/3rd the length of the hook shank between the tail and the wings (not the entire hook shank!).

7. Wrap the peacock herl up to this point, and then tie in a length of red floss.
8. Wrap up another 1/3rd of the body length with the thread (over the strand of peacock herl) and then cover this with a 1/3rd body length wrap of red floss.
9. Tie off the red floss and then wrap the thread forward the final 1/3rd of the body length.
10. Continue to wrap forward with the peacock herl to the thread, and then tie off and clip the excess herl.
11. Tie in a brown hackle or two, clip the butts and wind the hackle in front and in back of the previously tied wings. Tie down the hackle and clip the excess.
12. Make a neat head in front of the hackle them complete with a whip finish.
13. Seal the head with head cement.

GODDARD CADDIS

The deer-hair body to create the typical tent shape of the wing of caddis fly in this pattern makes it effective and a high-floater.

Tied by Chuck Edghill.

This tent-shaped adult winged caddis fly floats great as a result of the deer body hair used to make the wing and body. While really tied horizontal as a body would be, the result when trimmed is the shape of the caddis wing. This fly was introduced to this country by English angler John Goddard in his book *THE TROUT AND THE FLY*, which he co-authored with John Clarke. It is a high floater, as a result of the hollow deer body hair and is tied using the spinning technique of the Messinger Irresistible. As with that fly, you must trim the body before competing the fly, otherwise it would be easy to trim the hackle or antennae.

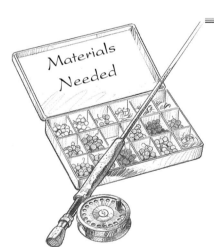

Materials Needed

Hook – Standard dry fly hook, sizes 10 to 14
Thread – Brown or black
Body – Tan deer body hair, spun and trimmed to shape
Antennae – Two stems of brown hackle, stripped
Hackle - Brown

Tying sequence:

1. Tie in the thread at the bend of the hook, and clip the excess thread.
2. Prepare bundles of tan or natural deer body hair, clipping closely to the skin, combing out the underfur and stacking. Tie the first bundle by holding it at an angle, then making soft loops over the bundle and hackle, and pull the thread to flare and spin the fur.
3. Push the spun bundle together with the thumb and fingernails of both hands, then repeat the above as necessary to fill the rear 2/3 of the hook shank with spun fur.
4. Half-hitch the thread, and then use scissors or a razor blade to trim the body/wing into a caddis wing tent shape, large at the rear and tapering smaller at the front. Trim flat on the bottom for maximum hook gap.

5. Once the body is shaped, tie in a pair of stripped stems of neck hackles to form the antennae. Make sure that they are of equal length and positioned properly on each side of the hook eye.
6. Tie in brown hackle and wrap the thread forward to just in back of the hook eye. Wrap the hackle around the hook shank to fill the space between the body/wing and the hook eye. Tie off the hackle end and cut the excess hackle. (An alternative to the above is to use the stems of the hackles as the antennae. For this, strip the lower end of the hackle, tie in place and then wrap the upper part of the hackle around the hook shank and tie off.)
7. Make a small neat head, then complete with a whip finish and cut the thread.
8. Seal with head cement.

LIME TRUDE

Trude style flies combine some classic trout patterns with the swept wing of a streamer, all on a standard or slightly long-shanked dry fly hook.

This fly has been a choice of anglers fishing the Jackson Hole One-Fly Contest, in which anglers have one fly and have to fish with it only. Fly choice is important, since once the fly is lost the game is over. With its shape and color, it might work as a suggestive simulation of a large stonefly or salmon fly. It is a good searching fly, fished on a cross-stream cast and drifted, then swung downstream. The more subdued Yellow Trude is tied with an elk hair tail, yellow body and squirrel tail wing.

It can also be tied using Royal Coachman colors of peacock herl and red floss for the body in the Royal Trude, first tied as a joke on an oversized hook at the A. S. Trude Ranch at Island Park, Idaho 100 years ago.

Tied by Umpqua.

Hook – Standard dry fly hook, size 8 to 14
Thread – Black
Tail – Golden pheasant tippet
Body – Lime colored dubbing, body material or yarn
Wings - White calf tail
 Hackle – Brown and grizzly, mixed

Tying sequence:

1. Tie in the thread at the bend of the hook and clip the excess thread.
2. Tie in the tail, followed by the body material. Alternatively, wax the tying thread and add dubbing.
3. Wrap the thread forward (or the dubbing, if using it) followed by the body material, then tie off and clip the excess. If using dubbing, remove any excess.
4. Tie in the wing, secure, and clip off the forward butts.
5. Tie in a brown and grizzly hackle, and wind both separately around the hook shank to fully dress the fly.
6. Tie off the hackles, clip to remove the excess and make a neat head.
7. Tie off with a whip finish, and clip the excess.
8. Seal with head cement.

ELK HAIR CADDIS

This fly uses the hair of the wing to suggest the tent-shaped wing of the natural. The hollow hair makes it a light-floater.

Al Troth designed this pattern, which has evolved over the years to become one of the several standard caddis patterns. It is an ideal pattern for caddis flies that have the tent-shaped wings folded over their body. The hollow elk hair helps to float the fly, while giving a pronounced caddis-wing effect to the fly. It can be dead floated, twitched to simulate the action of caddis flies as they touch the water, and skittered along the surface to simulate the "take-off" of the live insects.

Tied by Spirit River.

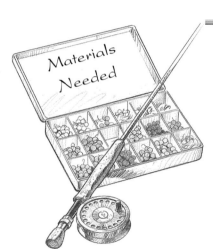

Materials Needed

Hook – Standard dry fly hook in sizes 10 to 20
Thread – Brown or tan
Rib – Furnace or brown hackle palmered through the body
Body – Hare's ear and mask fur dubbing
Wing - Tan colored elk hair fibers
Head – Trimmed butts of the elk hair wing, forward of the tie-down point.

Tying sequence:

1. Tie in the thread at the bend of the hook shank. Clip the excess thread.
2. Tie in the ribbing (palmering) hackle by the tip end and trim the excess.
3. Wrap the thread forward to the midpoint on the hook shank and tie in the dubbing or prepare the dubbing on the tying thread.
4. Wrap the thread to just in back of the hook eye. (Only if using dubbing separate from the tying thread.)
5. Wrap the dubbing up and down the hook shank to build up the body, then tie off in back of the hook eye, leaving enough room to tie in the elk hair and still tie off the fly.
6. Wrap the palmering hackle forward around the body and tie off at the thread position. Clip the excess hackle.
7. Place a small amount of elk hair in a hair evener (hair stacker) to position the hair ends. Remove and tie on top of the hook shank as a wing. Make several wraps to secure the elk hair, which will slightly flare up as a result of the hair being hollow.
8. Trim the forward ends of the elk hair to make a bulky, squared head.
9. Tie off with a whip finish on top of the elk hair windings or bring the thread forward on the hook shank and tie off with a whip finish on the bare hook shank.
10. Trim the excess butt ends of the elk hair to make a head.
11. Seal with head cement, taking care to seal the windings holding the elk hair in place.

COMPARADUN

The lack of hackle in the Comparadun, like that of the Haystack, makes this fly float in the surface film and more like the float of the natural dun mayfly.

The Comparadun is just what the name that author Al Caucci indicates – a fly designed to imitate a dun form of mayfly, and that invites comparison with the natural. It is tied without hackle, but with deer body hair in the flared wing to help it float and to make it sit in the surface film like the real fly. It is a variation of the previously developed Haystack, but comes in a variety of styles, emerger patterns, colors and designs to make for a whole family of flies. This pattern is basic, although with a trailing shuck instead of a tail to suggest a mayfly leaving its nymphal exoskeleton, it becomes a Sparkle Dun. In addition, Comparaduns and Sparkle Duns can be tied in a variety of ways for different fishing situations.

Tied by Umpqua.

Materials Needed

Hook – Standard dry fly hook, sizes 12 through 20
Thread – Brown
Tail – Splayed dark dun hackle fibers
Body – Brown dubbing, or brown dubbing-like body material
Wings - Deer hair tied upright, but flared to a 180-degree angle to help the fly float and stay upright

Tying sequence:

1. Tie in the thread about 1/3rd back from the hook eye, and clip the excess thread.
2. Tie in a bundle of deer hair for the wing, after first clipping, combing and stacking it. Tie with the tips forward, then raise a little of the bundle each time and wind the thread through to raise the entire wing to an upright position. Use your thumb to flare the wing out to the side to make it a 180-degree angle.
3. Tie over the butt end of the wing, then wrap the thread to the bend of the hook.
4. Tie in the tails, and make sure that they are splayed and divided. The best way to divide them is with a small ball of dubbing tied in before the tails are tied down.

5. Tie in the body material or add dubbing to the thread and wrap up the body and around the wings to tie off in back of the hook eye. (If using separate body material, wrap the thread forward, then follow with the body material and tie off in front of the wings in back of the hook eye.)
6. Tie off or remove excess dubbing, clip any excess body material and then tie a neat head.
7. Finish with a whip finish and clip the excess thread.
8. Seal with head cement.

DARBEE TWO-FEATHER MAYFLY

This simple, light and effective dry fly requires only two hackles to tie.

This simple fly was developed by Northeast angler Harry Darbee, and involves only two feathers or hackles. Darbee is also famous for developing the blue dun hackle color by breeding roosters that in many cases became the brood stock for the blue dun hackle available today. This fly is the epitome of a simple tie and also one that is very lightweight while forming the shape and silhouette of an extended-body mayfly. The one feather forms the tail and the silhouette of the body, while the second forms the hackle to help the fly ride upright.

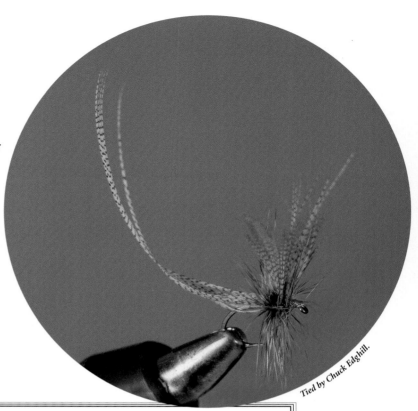

Tied by Chuck Edghill.

Materials Needed

Hook – Standard dry fly hook in sizes 12 through 16
Thread – Brown or black
Tail, Body and Wings – Carefully chosen symmetrical grizzly or dun hackle feather. Can also be tied using mallard or teal.
Hackle – Brown, dun or grizzly hackle

Tying sequence:

1. Tie in the thread about 1/3rd in back of the hook eye and clip the excess thread.
2. Prepare the tail by clipping out the final tip fibers, leaving two fibers on each side and then pulling the remainder of the fibers forward to form a translucent body silhouette.
3. Tie this pulled-forward tail and body to the hook shank with the concave side up to simulate the natural curvature of a mayfly body and tail. Use the remaining feather to tie in and divide the fan wings, formed by the fibers on each side of the body. Clip the excess part of the feather forward of this.
4. Tie in a hackle, clip the butt end and wind the hackle around the hook shank in front of and in back of the wings. Tie off and clip and excess hackle.
5. Make a small neat head, tie off with a whip finish and clip the excess thread.
6. Seal with head cement.

Wet Flies

BLACK GNAT

This is the wet fly version of the Black Gnat dry fly, and is tied similarly except for the hackle style.

Gnats are never as large as the Black Gnat wet fly fished by trout anglers. Basically, it is a black wet fly that to a trout might imitate any number of dark aquatic insects or dark colored terrestrials that fall into the water. Possibilities of the natural it might simulate include ants, crickets, any of the mayfly, stonefly or caddis fly nymphs, damsel or dragonfly nymphs, flies or wasps. No matter. It is still a great searching or explorer fly for cross-stream and downstream casting when trying new water or just searching for trout on older, well-known beats. The pattern below is one version. Other versions include a red butt and red hackle tail.

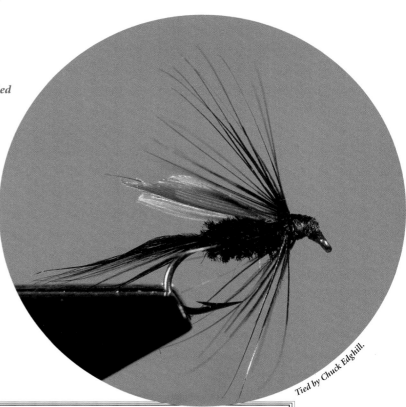

Tied by Chuck Edghill.

Hook – Wet fly hook, 1X or 2X stout, in sizes 8 to 14
Thread – Black
Tail – Black hackle fibers
Body – Black fur dubbing, black yarn or black chenille
Wings - Slate mallard wing quill sections
Hackle – Black hen hackle

Tying sequence:

1. Tie in the thread at the midpoint of the hook shank and clip any excess thread.
2. Wrap the thread to the bend of the hook and tie in the tail of black hackle fibers.
3. Tie down the body material of chenille, yarn or add black fur dubbing to the waxed tying thread.
4. Wind the thread forward to just in back of the hook eye, followed by wrapping the body material. Tie off the body material and remove (dubbing) or clip (yarn or chenille) the excess.
5. Tie in a black hackle fiber and clip the butt end. Wind the hackle around the hook shank, with the hackle in a flared back position – not upright as with dry flies.
6. Tie off the hackle, and trim any excess.
7. Select matched primary wing feathers and cut out sections to make the wings. Match the wing sections with the concave sides facing each other and tie down over the hackle. Clip the excess from in front of the tie and then complete a neat tapered head.
8. Complete with a whip finish, and clip the excess thread.
9. Seal with head cement.

GRAY NYMPH

Many of the Gray or Muskrat Nymphs tied today have tails, but this one seems to work just as effectively.

As a small boy, I was introduced to trout fishing and to this fly at the same time. It is simple, and not like most that you will find in books of trout flies. It is more wet fly than true nymph, thus its listing here. As a suggestive imitative type of fly, it could be any of a number of gray aquatic insects, nymphs, or even food washed into the trout stream. I like it best tied with mohair or leech yarn in a blue dun gray or light gray color. You could tie the same simple fly in a number of colors, with possibilities including black, white, yellow, cream, brownish orange, brown, tan, olive, and green. In recent years, I have also done well with it tied as a bead-head design. It is the same fly, just with the weight of a metal bead on the front end that helps to get it down, and gives it a jigging action when twitched or retrieved. A more standard version of this boyhood favorite fly has a badger guard hair tail.

Tied by the author.

Hook – Standard wet fly style, sizes 8 through 16
Thread – Gray or black
Body – Gray or blue dun gray mohair or Leech Yarn
Hackle – Blue dun or grizzly

Tying sequence:

1. Tie in the thread at the midpoint on the hook shank and clip off any excess thread.
2. Tie in the body material and wrap the thread forward to just in back of the hook eye.
3. Wrap the body material up to the thread, then down to the bend of the hook, then back up to the thread again. Tie off and clip the excess body material.
4. Choose a soft blue dun or grizzly hackle, trim the butt end and tie down to the hook shank. Trim any excess and wind the hackle around the hook shank, flared back, wet fly style.
5. Tie off with the thread and clip any excess hackle.
6. Wrap a neat head and complete the fly with a whip finish. Clip the excess thread.
7. Seal with head cement.

LIGHT CAHILL

Many flies are tied in both dry fly and wet fly styles.
This is one that is popular.

This fly, along with its companion Dark Cahill, is ideal respectively for cream/yellow and olive/brown aquatic insects. They are particularly good during most of the many mayfly hatches that occur throughout the angling year. It is another good fly to use as a searching or explorer fly for trying new water or revisiting old water.

Tied by the author.

Hook – Standard wet fly hook, sizes 10 to 16
Thread – Yellow or cream
Tail – Wood duck flank fibers or light ginger hen hackle fibers
Body – Cream fur dubbing or dubbing yarn
Wings - Wood duck flank fibers or lemon dyed mallard
Hackle – Ginger hen or cream hackle

Tying sequence:

1. Tie in the thread at the midpoint of the hook shank and clip any excess thread.
2. Wrap the thread to the bend of the hook and tie in the tail.
3. Then tie in the body material, and wrap the thread forward to in back of the hook eye or add dubbing to waxed tying thread.
4. Tie off the body and clip the excess or remove the excess dubbing.
5. Prepare a cream or ginger hen hackle, tie it in and clip the butt end. Wind the hackle around the hook shank, with the hackle in a flared back position – not upright as with dry flies.
6. Tie down the hackle and clip off the excess.
7. Prepare a wing of wood duck flank fibers and tie down on top of the hook shank, just in back of the hook eye. Trim the excess hackle.
8. Tie a neat head and finish the fly with a whip finish. Clip the excess thread.
9. Seal with head cement.

DARK CAHILL

A dark version of the Cahill style.

The Dark Cahill is another of those wet flies that along with the Light Cahill will match many underwater nymphs and available trout food. Together with the Light Cahill, you have two flies that will serve well as explorer flies for most trout waters, East and West. Other possibilities for such a light/dark series of wet flies are the Light Hendrickson and Dark Hendrickson, or a Ginger Wingless Wet and Blue Dun Wingless Wet.

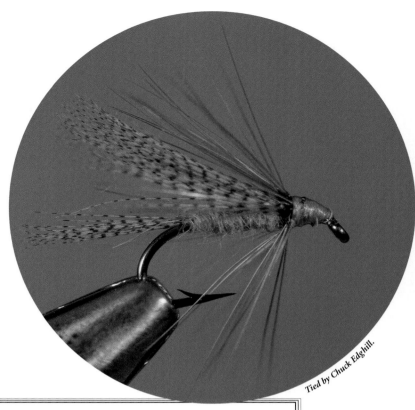

Tied by Chuck Edghill.

Hook – Standard wet fly hook, 1X to 2X stout if possible, in sizes 10 to 16
Thread – Black or dark brown
Tail – Furnace, dark brown hen hackle fibers, or wood duck
Body – Dark gray muskrat fur dubbing or similar synthetic dubbing
Hackle – Furnace or dark brown
Wings - Wood duck flank fibers or lemon dyed mallard

Tying sequence:

1. Tie in the thread at the midpoint of the hook shank and clip any excess thread.
2. Wrap the thread to the bend of the hook and tie in the tail.
3. Tie in the body material, and wrap the thread forward to in back of the hook eye or add dubbing to waxed tying thread.
4. Tie off the body and clip the excess or remove the excess dubbing.
5. Prepare a collar hackle, tie it in and clip the butt end.
6. Wind the hackle around the hook shank, with the hackle in a flared back position – not upright as with dry flies.
7. Tie down the hackle and clip off the excess.
8. Prepare a wing of wood duck flank fibers and tie down on top of the hook shank, just in back of the hook eye. Trim the excess hackle.
9. Tie a neat head and finish the fly with a whip finish. Clip the excess thread.
10. Seal with head cement.

LEADWING COACHMAN

Peacock herl seems to have a lot of attraction for trout, with many wet flies and nymphs including this material. This is one effective example.

This is a very dark wet fly, with the advantage of a lot of sparkle and buggy look as a result of the peacock herl body. Dave Hughes in his writings suggests using this fly when you see gray caddis in the air, since this can serve as a searching imitation of caddis that are on the bottom, or rising through the water column and not yet reaching the surface.

Tied by Chuck Edghill.

Hook – Wet fly hook, 1X or 2X stout, in sizes 10 through 14
Thread – Black
Tag – Narrow gold Mylar tinsel (traditional, but silver has also been used)
Rib – Narrow gold Mylar tinsel or wire is traditional, but silver has also been used. (It may not show with peacock herl.)
Body – Peacock herl
Hackle – Furnace or brown hen
Wings - Mallard quill or slate gray goose

Tying sequence:

1. Tie in the thread at midpoint on the hook shank.
2. Wrap the thread tightly toward the bend of the hook, and tie in the Mylar tinsel.
3. Wrap the thread forward a fraction of an inch and then wrap the tinsel forward to create the tag. Tie off the tinsel but do not clip the excess.
4. Follow by tying in two or three strands of peacock herl.
5. Wrap the thread forward, followed by the wrap of peacock herl. Tie off and clip any excess herl.
6. Spiral-wrap the tinsel over the body to form a ribbing and tie off. Then clip the excess.
7. Tie in the hackle, clip the excess and wind around the hook shank, flared back wet fly style. Tie off and clip the excess hackle.
8. Prepare and tie down the wing of goose or mallard. Clip any excess forward of the thread tie.
9. Finish with a neat head and tie off with a whip finish.
10. Seal with head cement.

OLIVE WET

A basic, easy-to-tie wet fly that takes a lot of trout at all levels of the water column.

This is another favorite fly from my youth, and much like the gray nymph described elsewhere. As such, it is a generic style that can be tied in any color using these basic materials of tag, body, wing and hackle. In many cases, I even leave the tag off, since the main attraction of this fly comes from its olive color and the general buggy appearance. Olive is a great color for all wet flies and nymphs. Depending upon the situation, you can fish this as a nymph on a dead drift and using a strike indicator, or as a wet fly, cast across or slightly downstream and swung in the current. Both work, with the dead drift best for pools and the swung fly best in pool tailwaters and riffles.

Tied by the author

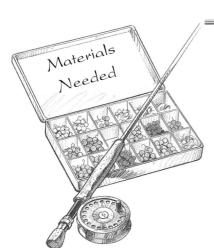

Hook – Standard wet fly hook in sizes 8 through 16
Tag – Flat gold tinsel (optional)
Body – Olive yarn or dubbing
Wing – Brown or slate wing quill
Hackle – Tan or brown

Tying sequence:

1. Tie the working thread onto the hook shank just above the bend of the hook.
2. Cut the tinsel at an angle, then tie down with the thread.
3. Wind the tinsel down the bend for a few turns, then reverse the tie back to the thread and tie off. Clip any excess tinsel.
4. Tie in the body material of yarn or add dubbing to the thread using the single strand or dubbing loop method.
5. Wrap the dubbing forward or if using separate material or a dubbing loop, wrap the thread forward to a spot about 1/4 back from the hook eye, followed by the yarn or dubbing.

6. Tie off the dubbing or yarn, or remove excess dubbing from the working thread, depending upon the method used.
7. Tie down the paired wings using the soft loop method, and clip excess wing material from in front of the tie-down point.
8. Prepare a hackle, strip the butt 1/4 inch and tie down with the working thread.
9. Wind the hackle around the hook shank, then tie off with the working thread and clip the excess hackle tip.
10. Use the thread to flare the hackle back, wet fly style, then form a neat head.
11. Tie off with a whip finish and seal with head cement.

ALDER

Many wet fly patterns, such as the Alder, originated in the New England area but will take trout anywhere.

This is primarily a New England pattern that is a derivation of an old English style and pattern. It is another of the many nymphs and wet flies tied with peacock herl that is always a good body material for its life-like sparkle and dark olive buggy appearance. This fly first debuted in this country in the early 1900s and today remains a staple and stable pattern for early spring fishing in the Northeast.

Tied by the author.

Materials Needed

Hook – Standard wet fly hook in sizes 8 to 14
Thread – Black
Tag – Flat gold tinsel
Body – Peacock herl
Wings - Mottled turkey wing quill sections
Hackle – Black

Tying sequence:

1. Tie in the thread at the midpoint on the hook shank, then wrap to the bend of the hook. Clip any excess thread.
2. Tie in the flat gold tinsel for the tag, then wrap the thread evenly forward for a few turns.
3. Wrap the tinsel evenly forward to form a tag and tie off. Clip the excess tinsel.
4. Tie in the peacock herl, then wrap the thread forward to just in back of the hook eye.
5. Follow with the wrap of peacock herl and tie off, then clip the excess peacock.
6. Prepare the hackle, either as fibers for a throat hackle or tie in a hackle to wind as a collar. Tie down the hackle, or wind the hackle around the hook shank and then tie off. Clip any excess.
7. Prepare the wing quill sections, position and tie down with thread. Clip any excess.
8. Wrap to make a neat head, then tie off with a whip finish, and clip the excess thread.
9. Seal with head cement.

PROFESSOR

Just as classic dry fly patterns are of the same style, but with different materials, so also are many wet flies. This is an example of an early simple wet fly.

This is another old attractor pattern, based on the early brook trout fishing in the East, and the fact that brook trout like bright attractor flies. It is a classic fly to fish with a downstream cast, making the cast quartering across the river, then allowing the fly to swing in the current through the best lies. Changing line length or casting position allows complete coverage of the water.

Tied by the author.

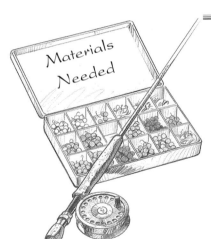

Hook – Standard wet fly, sizes 8 through 14
Thread – Black
Tag – Flat gold tinsel (optional)
Tail – Red Hackle fibers, dyed
Body – Yellow floss
Ribbing – Flat gold tinsel
Wings - Mallard flank fibers
Hackle – Brown, tied collar or throat style

Tying sequence:

1. Tie in the thread at the midpoint on the fly, then clip the excess and wrap the thread to the bend of the hook.
2. Tie in the tinsel for the tag and wrap forward several even wraps of thread.
3. Wrap the tinsel forward and tie off. Do not clip.
4. Tie in the tail fibers followed by the body floss.
5. Wrap the thread forward to in back of the hook eye.
6. Wrap the floss forward to form the body, then tie off and clip the excess.
7. Spiral wrap the tinsel forward to form the ribbing. Tie off and clip the excess.
8. Tie in the throat or collar hackle – if collar, wind around the hook shank and tie off. Clip any excess.
9. Prepare and position the wing fibers on the hook, and tie down. Clip any excess.
10. Make a neat head, then tie off with a whip finish and clip the excess thread.
11. Seal with head cement.

PARTRIDGE AND GREEN

Soft-hackle flies, with simple bodies, often lacking wings and with long soft hackle from game birds, have recently become effective and are very popular.

The Partridge and Green is a traditional soft hackle wet fly, and similar to the Partridge and Orange that differs only by having brown partridge and an orange body. These are classic wet flies, with this soft hackle concept first written about by Dame Juliana Berners in her *TREATISE OF FISHING WITH AN ANGLE*, published in 1496. Sylvester Nemes re-popularized soft-hackle flies with his several books on the subject. These soft-hackle flies vary from standard wet flies in that they have longer, softer hackle that is sparse and which veils the fly, rather than the cone-like collar of a wrapped hackle or the bristly moustache appearance of a throat hackle. As a result, they have far more action in the water and look and act buggy to imitate a number of downed and drowned insects, including mayflies and caddis flies.

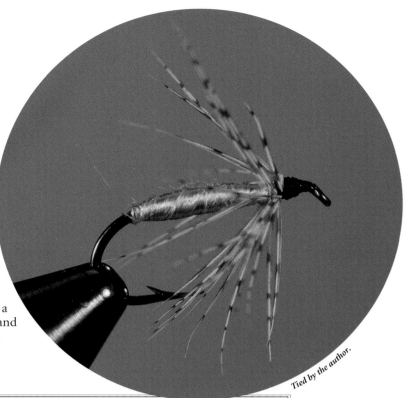

Tied by the author.

Materials Needed

Hook – Standard wet fly hook, sizes 10 through 16
Thread – Black
Body – Bright green
Hackle – Gray partridge

Tying sequence:

1. Tie in the thread at the midpoint on the hook shank, clip the excess thread and then wrap evenly to the bend of the hook.
2. Tie in the floss and wrap the thread forward to in back of the hook eye.
3. Wrap the floss forward to form a body, tie off and clip the excess.
4. Tie in a long, soft partridge hackle, wrap two or three turns (it should be sparse) and tie off. Clip the excess, make a neat head and tie off with a whip finish. Clip the excess thread.
5. Seal with head cement.

GRIZZLY KING

Older wet flies are often more colorful and bright than the newer and currently popular patterns, but still take their share of trout.

The Grizzly King is another famous wet fly, originating in New England waters where it was developed early on for brook trout fishing. It is also proving excellent for fishing Western waters, and bridges the gap between attractor and imitative flies. The green floss, ribbing and red tail make it more of an attractor, but the slim shape, mallard flank wings and grizzly hackle throat make it a suggestive imitation of a number of both land-based and aquatic insects.

Tied by the author.

Materials Needed

Hook – Standard wet fly hook, sizes 8 through 14
Thread – Black
Tail – Red hackle fibers
Body – Bright green floss
Ribbing – Flat silver or gold tinsel
Wings – Mallard flank fibers
Hackle – Grizzly

Tying sequence:

1. Tie in the thread at the midpoint on the fly, then clip the excess and wrap the thread to the bend of the hook.
2. Tie in the tail fibers followed by the tinsel ribbing and then the body floss.
3. Wrap the thread forward to in back of the hook eye.
4. Wrap the floss forward to form the body, then tie off and clip the excess.
5. Spiral wrap the tinsel forward to form the ribbing. Tie off and clip the excess.
6. Tie in the throat hackle and clip the butts.
7. Prepare and position the wing fibers on the hook, and tie down. Clip any excess.
8. Make a neat head, then tie off with a whip finish and clip the excess thread.
9. Seal with head cement.

MONTREAL

This fly, with the turkey wing, is more imitative of natural flies than many early wet flies.

The Montreal is another good wet fly pattern that, with its speckled turkey wing and red body with gold ribbing, combines features of both attractor and simulator patterns. As the name indicates, it is basically a Canadian pattern that dates from about 1840. It will work well for trout everywhere, however. It is an ideal attractor fly when fishing pockets and pools in a systematic searching pattern to find trout.

Tied by the author.

Materials Needed

Hook – Standard wet fly hook, sizes 8 through 12
Thread – Black
Tail – Red hackle fibers
Body – Purplish-red or claret floss
Ribbing – Flat gold tinsel
Wings - Speckled turkey quill or speckled hen quill segments
Hackle – Purplish red or dark red (claret) hen, tied collar or throat style

Tying sequence:

1. Tie in the thread at the midpoint of the hook, clip the excess and wrap to the bend of the hook.
2. Tie in the tail fibers, then tie in the ribbing of gold tinsel
3. Tie in the floss body, then wrap over the tag ends of the tails, tinsel and floss to the tie-down point in back of the hook eye.
4. Wrap the floss body forward, tapering it in the process. Tie the floss off and clip the excess.
5. Spiral wrap the tinsel ribbing forward, then tie off at the thread and clip the excess.
6. Tie in the hackle, trim the butt end, then wind the

hackle around the hook shank so that the hackle will flare back.
7. Tie down the end of the hackle and clip the excess. (Alternatively, tie in a throat hackle.)
8. Tie in the wings, position them carefully on top of the hook shank and trim the butt ends.
9. Wrap the area with thread to make a tapered head, then complete with a whip finish and clip the excess thread.
10. Seal with head cement.

PICKET PIN

The palmered hackle and flared back wing of this fly makes it cross between a streamer and wet fly.

The Picket Pin is another of those flies tied with palmered hackle and a swept back wing that can be fished dry, wet or like a streamer. It is similar in design and tying to the Improved Sofa Pillow or the Stimulator. Since it does not have deer or elk hair in the wing, nor a collar hackle, this form is fished wet like a wet fly or nymph. Since it has peacock herl, a popular body material for wet flies, it is an effective and lifelike fly that accounts for a lot of trout.

Tied by Chuck Edghill.

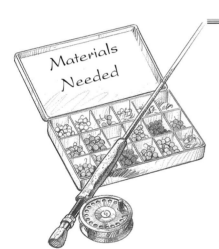

Materials Needed

Hook – Nymph hook, 2x or 3X long, in sizes 6 through 12
Thread – Black
Tail – Brown hackle fibers
Body – Peacock herl
Wings - Gray squirrel tail
Hackle – Brown hackle, palmered over the body
Head – Peacock herl

Tying sequence:

1. Tie in the thread at the bend of the hook, clip the excess and then tie in the tail fibers.
2. Clip the excess tail fibers, then tie in a brown hackle by the tip.
3. Tie in enough peacock herl to form the body.
4. Wrap the thread forward to in back of the hook eye, (about 1/4 of the hook shank length in back), then follow with the peacock herl.
5. Tie off the peacock herl. If you have some herl remaining, do not clip.
6. Palmer (spiral wrap) the hackle forward and tie off at the thread position. Clip any excess hackle.

7. Prepare (clip, comb and stack) a bundle of squirrel tail, and tie in place as a wing. Clip the forward butts.
8. Wrap the thread forward to the hook eye.
9. Continue the wrap with the peacock herl, or tie in more peacock, then wrap the thread forward and follow with a wrap of peacock.
10. Tie off, then clip the excess herl, make a head and tie off the fly with a whip finish. Clip the excess thread.
11. Seal with head cement.

PARMACHENE BELLE

The only part of this fly that is difficult is joining or marrying the white and red wing sections.

This colorful fly was named for Lake Parmachene in Maine and is an old pattern. As such, it is a bright attractor pattern that also incorporates a method of making quill wings of different colors, married together by mating the barbules of the barbs or separate fibers. This same technique of marrying the white, red and white of the wing can be used on any fly or bright attractor pattern to make wings of any combination of colors using duck quill sections.

Tied by the author.

Hook – Standard wet fly hook, sizes 8 to 12
Thread – Black
Tail – Red and white hackle fibers, mixed
Body – Yellow floss
Ribbing – Flat gold tinsel
Wings – Married strips of duck quill sections, white, then red, then white
Hackle – Mixed dyed red and white hackle

Tying sequence:

1. Tie in the thread at the mid point on the fly, clip the excess thread, then wrap the thread to the bend of the hook.

2. Tie in the red and white tail fibers, then tie in the flat gold tinsel, followed by the yellow floss body material.

3. Wrap the thread forward over the excess floss and tail fibers, to a point slightly in back of the hook eye.

4. Wrap the floss forward to form a body and tie off at the thread. Clip the excess thread.

5. Spiral wrap the ribbing forward and tie off and the thread. Clip the excess.

6. Tie in red and white hackle fibers under the fly to make a throat hackle.

7. Prepare wing quill sections of white and red by marrying the sections together to make the white/red/white wing for each side.

8. Tie the wings down in place and clip the excess.

9. Make a neat head, then tie off with a whip finish and clip the excess thread.

10. Seal with head cement.

WOODCOCK AND ORANGE

Most soft-hackle patterns are simply body and hackle, and very easy to tie and fish.

This is another of the many soft-hackle flies available, and ideal for fishing in a downstream cast, allowing the fly to roll and drift in the current of small fast runs where trout have to take a fly quickly or not get it at all. As with the Partridge and Green, this fly is made of the soft hackle fibers from game birds. While woodcock is used, it should be just as effective using brown partridge or other soft hackle, including soft hen hackle from chickens.

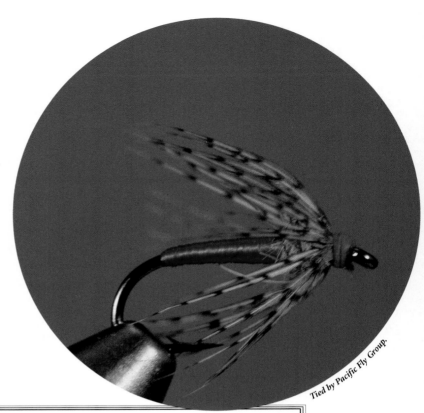

Tied by Pacific Fly Group.

Materials Needed

Hook – Standard wet fly hook, sizes 12 to 16
Thread – Brown
Body – Orange floss
Hackle – Brown woodcock body feather, or brown soft hen hackle or brown partridge.

Tying sequence:

1. Tie in the thread at the midpoint on the hook shank, clip the excess thread and then wrap evenly to the bend of the hook.
2. Tie in the floss and wrap the thread forward to in back of the hook eye.
3. Wrap the floss forward to form a body, tie off and clip the excess.
4. Tie in a long, soft hackle, wind two or three turns (it should be sparse) and tie off. Clip the excess, make a neat head and tie off with a whip finish. Clip the excess thread.
5. Seal with head cement.

McGINTY

This bee pattern is effective for trout, since bees are known to elicit strikes when they fall into streams.

The McGinty is one of those flies that will work everywhere, at any level of the water column, even through it imitates a bumblebee with the alternate bands of yellow and black chenille. While few bumblebees probably fall into the water, this fly works as another of the colorful attractor patterns. Obviously, it is best as an imitative fly during the summer months when worker bees are out. It is particularly good around lowlands and pastures with flowers that are frequently visited by bees.

Tied by Holly Flies.

Hook – Standard wet fly hook, sizes 8 to 12
Thread – Black
Tail – Mixed dyed red hackle fibers and barred teal flank fibers
Body – Bands of black and yellow chenille
Wings – White-tipped mallard secondary wing quill sections
Hackle – Brown

Tying sequence:

1. Tie in the thread at the bend of the hook, then clip the excess thread.
2. Tie in the tail, first with the red hackle, over which is tied the teal fibers.
3. Tie in the yellow chenille, followed by the black chenille.
4. Wrap the thread forward, followed by one wrap of black chenille wrapped over the yellow.
5. Tie off the black chenille and wrap the thread forward again, followed by one wrap of the yellow chenille wrapped over the black.
6. Tie off and clip the yellow chenille, then wrap the thread forward, followed by a wrap of the black chenille.
7. Tie off the black chenille and clip the excess.
8. Tie in a brown throat or collar hackle, tying in the fibers or tying in the hackle and then wrapping it around the hook shank. Clip the butt fibers or the excess hackle.
9. Prepare the white-tipped wing quills and tie in place, then clip the excess butt ends.
10. Tie a neat head, then tie off with a whip finish and clip the excess thread.
11. Seal with head cement.

Nymphs

GOLD-RIBBED HARE'S EAR

This widely known and most popular nymph is a basic for any trout fly box.

Eric Leiser, in his book, *THE BOOK OF FLY PATTERNS*, refers to this pattern as "the American Express card in the nymph category of flies. You don't want to go astream without it." It is a basic nymph that over the years has accounted for a huge number of trout catches on waters everywhere. The very fact that it has been around for so long, and still remains so popular, attests to its continued effectiveness. It is a basic pattern that you will find in almost all books on flies, almost all recommendations for nymph fishing and in almost all fly boxes.

Tied by Chuck Edghill.

Materials Needed

Hook – 1X to 2X long nymph hook, 1X to 2X stout, in sizes 10 to 16
Weight – Light lead or non-lead wire, about ten turns, centered on the shank
Thread – Black
Tail – Guard hairs from hare's mask
Ribbing – Oval gold tinsel
Abdomen – Tan dubbing, hare's mask fur
Wing case – Mottled turkey tail feather
Thorax – Blended hare's mask

Tying sequence:

1. Tie on the thread at the bend of the hook and clip the excess thread. Wrap the hook shank with ten or so wraps of lead or non-lead wire.
2. Tie in a hare's mask guard hair tail, using the hairs from the ears or cheek area.
3. Tie in the gold tinsel, and trim the excess, followed by a tie of dubbing secured to the waxed tying thread. Wrap the thread (dubbing) forward, or wrap the thread forward, followed by the dubbing loop. Clip or remove the excess dubbing.
4. Spiral wrap the tinsel forward to rib the abdomen. Tie off and clip the excess.
5. Tie in a section of turkey tail feather for the wing case and then tie in the dark brown dubbing or add the dubbing to the waxed tying thread.
6. Wrap the dark brown thorax forward with the thread or following the thread. Tie off and clip the excess.
7. Fold over the turkey wing case and tie down, then clip the excess.
8. Make a neat head, then whip finish, clip the excess thread.
9. Seal with head cement.

PHEASANT TAIL NYMPH

Many simple nymphs are far more effective than the complex patterns available. This is an example of a relatively simple tie.

The Pheasant Tail Nymph was first tied in England by Frank Sawyer, and developed for the chalk stream fishing there. It is a welcome immigrant to this country, particularly as more and more attention has been placed on spring creeks and limestone waters. Various authors have described the different recipes for this fly, some suggesting using copper wire as the tying thread as well as the ribbing; others suggesting using gold wire for the ribbing but tying with standard black tying thread. The wire tie gives the fly more weight, which often helps nymphs to get down to the right depth. Another way to achieve added weight is to use a stout hook in place of a standard nymph hook, or to add two strips of lead wire parallel to the hook before over-wrapping with the body and ribbing.

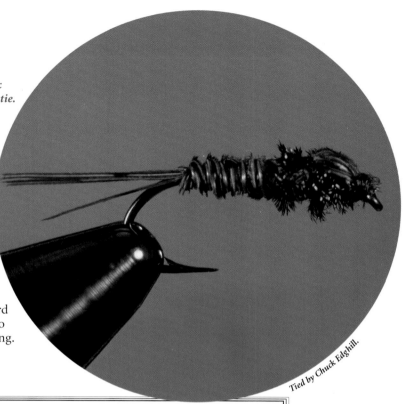

Tied by Chuck Edghill.

Materials Needed

Hook – 1X or 2X long nymph hook, 1X or 2X stout in sizes 10 to 18
Weight – Two strips of lead wire, the length of the hook shank, tied in on each side and parallel to the hook shank (optional)
Thread – Fine copper wire or black tying thread
Tail – Ringneck pheasant tail fibers
Body – Butts of the tail fibers, wrapped around the hook shank
Wing case – Butts and body of pheasant tail fibers
Thorax – Butts and body of pheasant tail fibers
Legs – Butt end of the thorax fibers

Tying sequence:

1. Tie in the thread or wire at the bend of the hook.
2. Wrap up and down the shank over the lead wire, if used for weight, returning to the bend of the hook.
3. Tie in the tail fibers, and wrap them forward to the midpoint of the hook shank. If using thread, wrap the thread forward first and then tie off at this point.
4. Overwrap the butts of the tail with the copper wire, counter wrapping around the hook shank,
5. Form a loop of pheasant tail and fold down and tie in place. The loop should extend to the rear of the fly.

6. Add more pheasant fibers at this point, tying down, then wrapping the fibers forward and counterwrapping with the copper wire.
7. Fold the loop of pheasant fibers over the thorax of the fly, and tie down. Fold the tip ends under the fly as a hackle throat.
8. Tie off with thread and whip finish or wrap with the copper wire to complete.
9. Seal with head cement.

BITCH CREEK NYMPH

Western trout fishermen often use larger nymphs that are suggestive of the nymphal life on their streams. This is a popular pattern everywhere, but particularly in Western waters.

The Bitch Creek nymph is a standard rubber-legged salmon fly nymph imitation that was developed in Western waters and is primarily used there. It uses a method of "weaving" the two body materials around the hook to make a two-toned effect – orange on the bottom and black on top. There is another way to achieve this that is far simpler, however. To do this, tie in one strand of the orange, two short strands of the black chenille and a short length of copper or gold wire ribbing at the appropriate spot in the tying process. Leave the tag end of the working thread long where tied down at the bend of the hook. Then wrap the thread forward, followed by wrapping the orange chenille around the hook shank. Tie off the orange and then lay the two strands of black chenille over the back of the fly and tie down. Follow with a spiral ribbing wrap of the tag end of thread to hold the black chenille in place and tie it off also. The following pattern explains the weaving process, which is correct for this pattern, but more complicated to learn.

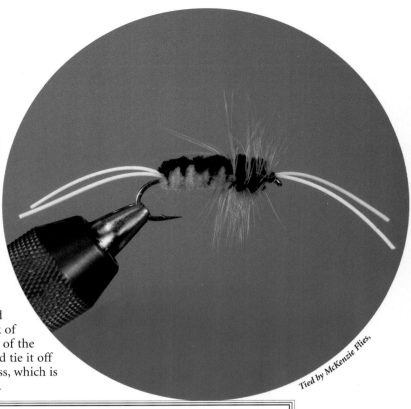

Tied by McKenzie Flies,

Materials Needed

Hook – Standard streamer or 2X long nymph hook in sizes 4 to 8
Weight – Lead or non-lead wire wrapped around the full length of the hook shank
Thread – Black
Tails – White rubber hackle
Abdomen – Woven black and orange chenille
Rib – Gold wire counterwound over the thorax hackle
Hackle – Brown, palmered
Thorax – Black chenille
Antennae – White rubber hackle

Tying sequence:

1. Tie in the thread at the bend of the hook, clip the excess, then wrap the shank with lead or non-lead wire.
2. Tie down a length of white rubber leg material, fold it over and tie so that it extends in back of the fly as a tail.
3. Tie down black and orange chenille and clip and excess. Wrap the thread forward to just ahead of the midpoint of the shank.
4. Make a complete reverse wrap of black chenille, then bring the orange chenille under the hook, around the black chenille – back to front – and pull under the fly to the back side (left side of the fly – back side as you look at the fly).
5. Bring the black chenille over the top of the hook and repeat the above, to bring the orange chenille around the black chenille and back to the near side of the fly. Bring the black over the top of the fly as before.

6. Repeat the above until reaching the thread, then tie off both and clip the orange chenille. Tie in the ribbing wire and a brown hackle and wrap the thread forward to in back of the hook eye.
7. Tie in the forward strand of white rubber leg, fold over to secure with thread.
8. Wrap the black chenille forward and tie off with the tying thread. Clip the excess chenille, then palmer wrap the hackle forward. Clip the excess hackle.
9. Counter wrap with the ribbing wire through and over the hackle to further secure it. Tie off the ribbing wire, and clip the excess.
10. Make a neat head and complete with a whip finish. Clip the excess thread.
11. Seal with head cement.

BEAD-HEAD PRINCE

Beads allow tiers to add color and weight to their nymphs. Depending upon the bead used, the weight allows the nymph to get deep, as it does on this basic trout nymph.

The Bead-head Prince nymph is a bead-head version of Prince Nymph, which is similar to the Zug Bug, another generic searching nymph-style of fly. The bead at the head gives the fly some weight to get it down a little more. It can be tied with or without lead wire on the hook shank, and for that matter, with or without the bead head. This pattern is with the bead head, but without the lead wire that is often added to these flies if lacking the brass or gold bead as the head. The bead head on this or any nymph allows giving it a unique up/down yo-yo action in the water that seems to be particularly appealing to trout.

Tied by Chuck Edgehill.

Hook – Standard nymph hook, 1X to 2X long, 1X or 2X stout, in sizes 12 to 18
Bead – Brass or gold, to fit
Thread – Black
Tail – Brown turkey biots, forked
Ribbing – Thin flat gold tinsel
Body – Peacock herl
Wings – White turkey biots
Hackle – Brown hen, sparse

Tying sequence:

1. Use pliers to bend down the barb of the hook and slip on an appropriate size brass or gold bead.
2. Tie the thread in back of the bead to help hold it in place while tying the rest of the fly. Trim the excess thread.
3. Wrap the thread to the tail, and tie in the turkey biots.
4. Tie in the ribbing of gold tinsel, then tie in the peacock herl.
5. Wrap the thread forward to a spot just in back of the bead.
6. Wrap the peacock herl forward and tie off with the thread. Clip any excess.
7. Spiral wrap the ribbing forward, counterwrapping it to help reinforce the peacock herl. Tie down and clip and excess.
8. Tie in a brown hackle, and trim the butt end. Make one or two turns of the hackle around the hook shank and tie off. Clip the excess hackle.
9. Tie in the forked white turkey biots parallel to the body. Trim any excess.
10. Make a whip finish to complete the fly and cut the excess thread.
11. Seal with head cement.

OLIVE BEAD-HEAD SCUD

Freshwater shrimp, sow bugs and scuds are an important trout food, of which this fast-sinking bead-head pattern is just one design.

Scuds can be tied in an almost generic style, using a bead head for weight, lead wire wrapped on the body for weight, or tied with no weight at all and weighted with split shot on the leader. Scuds are small shrimp-like creatures that can be found in a variety of colors and sizes and often even different shapes. This pattern can be used as a basic design, or template, and changed as above with weight or color.

Tied by Umpqua

Hook – 1X or 2X long nymph hook with model perfect bend (to receive bead) in sizes 12 through 18
Bead – Metal, black, dark, or bright to fit hook
Thread – Olive
Body – Olive dubbing or mohair
Rib – Tying thread, black
Shellback – Clear plastic poly bag strip

Tying sequence:

1. Bend down the barb of the hook, then use tweezers to slip on an appropriate size bead.
2. Tie in the tying thread at the tail of the hook, and leave a long tag end for making the ribbing later in the tying process or, tie down black thread.
3. Tie down a strip of plastic, usually no more than about 1/8 to 1/4 inch wide, depending upon the hook size.
4. Add wax to the tying thread, then add the olive dubbing.
5. Wrap the dubbing forward or wrap the thread forward followed by the body material. Tie off or remove any excess dubbing.

6. Fold the slip of plastic over the top of the fly, and use the tag end of the thread to spiral wrap or rib the fly body over the plastic shellback.
7. Tie off the thread and the plastic strip at the head of the fly, and clip off any excess.
8. Tie a neat head, then make a whip finish and clip the excess thread.
9. Seal with head cement and add some head cement to the shellback ribbing for added protection.

SERENDIPITY

Patterns that imitate flies that are in the emerging stage as they pop through the water surface are the latest theory in fly design. This fly, with the deer-hair wing, achieves that look as it floats in the surface film.

These little flies are credited by Dave Hughes to the late Ross Marigold, a Madison River guide. They are also similar to a British lake midge pattern called a buzzer. Serendipity patterns can be tied in a number of colors and with a number of materials to imitate almost anything. Tied with a length of a large bundle deer hair, they will swim under the surface like an emerger. Tied in small sizes and drifted on lakes and ponds, they will imitate a midge. With less and shorter clipped deer hair and fished on the bottom with split shot on the leader, they can imitate any small nymph. With their shape, they can also imitate beetles or scuds. This is an olive Serendipity, but it can also be tied in gray, tan, brown, light olive, black and other colors. It also can be tied in a bead-head form. While Antron or Z-lon are standard for this tie, more flash can be created by using twisted Krystal Flash or Crystal Splash in various colors.

Tied by McKenzie.

Materials Needed

Hook – Standard dry fly hook or a curved shank scud hook, sizes 14 to 22
Thread – Olive
Body – Olive Antron or Z-lon, twisted
Head and collar – Natural deer hair

Tying sequence:

1. Tie in the working thread in back of the eye, clip the excess and wrap the thread down to the hook bend.

2. Tie in a length of body material (Antron yarn, Z-lon, Krystal Flash or Crystal Splash) that when twisted will make a rope or noodle for wrapping around the hook shank.

3. Wrap the thread forward to about 1/4 inch back of the hook shank.

4. Twist the body material and wrap it around the hook shank. Note that the body material must be twisted again with each wrap of material to prevent the body rope from becoming untwisted.

5. Tie off at the thread position and clip the excess body material.

6. Prepare (clip, comb and stack) a small bundle of natural deer hair, then hold in position and tie down with two soft loops of thread.

7. Continue to wrap the thread through the deer hair, and try to hold the deer hair more in a stacked position than a completely encircling spun position.

8. Wrap the thread forward of the head and tie off with a whip finish. Clip the excess thread. Seal with head cement.

9. Trim the deer hair to make a small head with a slight collar extending in back and over the body.

10. (An alternative to the above last step is to tie down the deer hair, then trim it before completing with a whip finish. This makes it easier to make the whip finish but be careful to avoid cutting the thread.)

BROOKS MONTANA STONEFLY

For fishing deep through fast pools in Western trout streams, this fly is hard to beat.

Western trout writer Charles Brooks designed this fly. It is a basic for the big stoneflies that are found in Western waters, and as a heavily weighted fly, can be fished deep through the fast-flowing pools of Western rivers. It was developed as a result of Brooks' diving into trout streams and watching trout in their reaction to live stonefly nymphs and to various imitations. He found that trout shied away from two-tone nymphs as they turned and rolled in the current, and thus developed his theory of tying "in the round" so that the trout will see the same thing regardless of how the fly rolls or turns. Another version of this is the simplified Brooks Brown Stonefly. This is tied a golden brown color to imitate the golden stone fly nymph of Western waters. It is also an excellent heavily weighted nymph that is of a different color than the Montana Stonefly imitation, and thus effective for different waters and different situations. The dressing for the Montana Stonefly is:

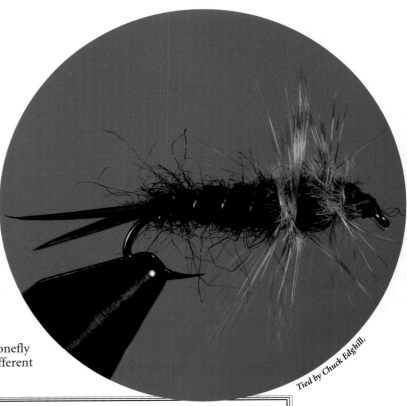

Tied by Chuck Edghill.

Materials Needed

Hook – 3X or 4X long nymph or standard streamer hook, sizes 4 to 8
Thread – Black
Weight – Lead or non-lead wire.
Tail – Black stripped goose, raven or crow wing quills
Body, Abdomen – Black yarn or black mohair
Body, Thorax – Black yarn or black mohair
Ribbing – Copper wire, spiral wrapped up over the abdomen, then wrapped over the hackle and herl gills/legs.
Legs – Mixed brown and grizzly hackle,
Gills – White or gray ostrich herl

Tying sequence:

1. Tie in the thread at the bend of the hook, clip the excess, then wrap the hook shank with lead or non-lead wire, double wrapping at the front 1/3rd of the fly.
2. Spiral wrap over the wire, then return to the rear and tie in the tail. Clip the excess and tie in the copper wire ribbing, then the black yarn body material.
3. Wrap the thread up to the double wire wrap, then follow with the body yarn and tie off.
4. Wrap the abdomen with the spiral copper wire ribbing and tie off. Do not clip either material.
5. Tie in the brown hackle, grizzly hackle and the ostrich herl. Wrap the thread to just in back of the hook eye.
6. Follow with the wrap of black yarn and tie off.
7. Wrap the brown hackle, grizzly hackle and ostrich herl together in a spiral wrap to the head and tie off with the working thread. Clip the excess materials.
8. Spiral wrap the copper wire ribbing forward over the hackle/herl, counter winding it to strengthen and reinforce the gills and legs. Clip the excess wire.
9. Make a neat head with the tying thread and complete the fly with a whip finish.
10. Seal with head cement.

OLIVE CADDIS

Caddis are less popular than mayflies, but still important trout food, particularly in the nymphal stage.

This is another caddis imitation, and while more typical of those that might be fished in the East, it is useful for any trout waters. It is a simple fly to tie, and can be tied in a number of sizes, based on the size of caddis in your trout waters. It helps to turn over a few rocks (turn them back when returning them to the water) to check on the color and size of caddis larva cases. This might also be taken by the trout as any of a number of nymphs. While the olive color is perhaps the best, most effective and most popular, it can also be tied in any color by just changing body color and retaining the peacock herl head. It is not included in this pattern, but it can also be fished weighted with lead or non-lead wire, or in a metallic bead-head style.

Tied by Brookside Flies.

Hook – 1X to 2X long nymph hook, 1X to 2X stout, in sizes 8 through 18

Thread – Black

Body – Olive fur dubbing, or olive yarn, frayed out to a diameter appropriate for the hook size. Over wrap with clear plastic strip.

Head – Peacock herl

Tying sequence:

1. Tie in the thread at the midpoint of the hook shank, then wrap it to the bend of the hook. Clip any excess thread.
2. Tie in the plastic strip and olive yarn (which I prefer) or add olive dubbing to the waxed tying thread. Wrap the thread or the dubbing forward to a point about 1/4 the shank length behind the hook eye.
3. Tie off the yarn and clip or remove any excess dubbing.
4. Spiral wrap the plastic strip forward and tie off.
5. Tie in the peacock herl.
6. Wrap the tying thread forward to just in back of the hook eye.
7. Wrap the peacock forward and tie off, then clip the excess.
8. Complete a neat head, then tie off with a whip finish and clip the excess thread.
9. Seal with head cement.

SAND CASE CADDIS

Since caddis live as nymphs in sand or stick cases, this is an easy-to-tie natural for them.

You will seldom find this dressing in fly-tying volumes, although it is an interesting and different imitation of the caddis larva. These larva make cases to surround and protect all but their head. Usually these cases are of sand, but sticks, twigs and vegetation are also used. Case design is often specific to a particular caddis species. This is more of a fly gluing project than one of fly-tying, although both techniques are involved. They are fun to play with and with the sand weight, will sink to the bottom where cased caddis are usually found. Ideally, they are best made using sand from the local stream where you plan to fish, assuming that removing a little sand for fly-tying is not illegal. The same technique can be used to tie (glue) flies using twigs, bits of leaves and detritus, since caddis use these materials also for building their cases.

Tied by the author.

Hook – 2X long, wet fly or nymph hook, 1X or 2X stout if possible, in sizes 8 through 12
Thread – Black
UnderBody – Thin layer of tan yarn. (Tan yarn is used in case any of the underbody shows through the sand case.)
Body – Dry river or stream sand, glued to the yarn underbody.
Head – Peacock herl

Tying sequence:

1. Tie in the working thread in back of the hook eye, and wrap it to the bend of the hook. Clip any excess thread.
2. Tie in the yarn and wrap the thread back up the hook to about 1/4 the shank length behind the head. Clip any excess yarn.
3. Wrap the yarn up the hook shank and tie off at the thread, clipping any excess yarn.
4. Tie in peacock herl. Wrap the peacock herl up to the hook eye and back down to the thread, then tie off and clip the excess peacock herl.
5. Complete the fly with a whip finish at this point (between the under body and head) and seal the whip finish with head cement.
6. The fly can be fished this way, since the tan yarn will simulate the caddis case. However, to complete the fly, coat and soak the yarn body (not the peacock herl) with thin waterproof glue, then roll the fly in dry sand so that the sand adheres to the underbody casing. Roll with your fingers to press the sand into the glue and to smooth the finish.

BRASSIE

The wire body of this fly makes it a sinker, which makes it so good.

This little fly, variously described as being developed in Colorado or the Southwest, is designed to imitate Western caddis larva that make their cases from reddish sand or sand with mica and minerals in it. Thus, the coloration is different from the light cream or tan colors of sand from most Eastern streams. The head can be tied of peacock herl or picked out gray-black fur dubbing. Because of the weight of the brass in the body, no other weight is required of this fly to roll it along the bottom.

Tied by McKenzie.

Hook – 2X long, 1X or 2X stout, wet fly hook in sizes 10 through 16
Thread – Black
Body – Brass wire, appropriate diameter to the size of the hook. Cooper or other metallic wires can also be used for a slightly different effect.
Head – Peacock herl or picked out black or gray dubbing.

Tying sequence:

1. Tie in the thread about 1/3rd the shank length in back of the eye, then wrap to the bend of the hook. Clip any excess thread.
2. Tie down the brass wire securely, and wrap over the tag end all the way back to 1/3rd the point in back of the eye.
3. Wrap the brass wire carefully up to the position of the thread and tie off. Clip the excess wire, using wire clippers or heavy scissors.
4. Tie in peacock herl or add black/gray fur or synthetic dubbing to the waxed tying thread.
5. Wrap the head material up to the head, back again and then up to the eye of the hook. Clip the peacock herl or remove the dubbing, then tie off with a small neat head.
6. Complete with a whip finish and clip the excess thread.
7. Seal with head cement.

TEENY NYMPH

This simple fly of one material is suggestive and very buggy looking in the water.

Jim Teeny, maker of the fast-sinking fly lines and other fly-fishing accessories, originated this fly. It was designed for lake fishing for trout in the Oregon area, but has gained a national reputation. It is one of those simple, but very effective buggy looking generic nymph patterns that sinks well as a result of the weighted body.

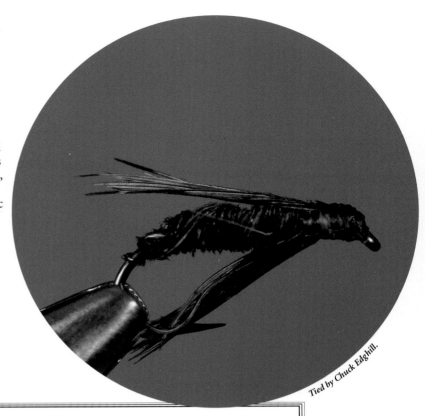

Tied by Chuck Edghill.

Hook – Wet fly hook in sizes 4 through 12
Thread – Black
Weight – Lead wire, wrapped around hook shank
Body – Bundle of natural or dyed ringneck pheasant tail fibers, wrapped around hook shank to form body
Legs – Remainder of the ringneck pheasant tail fibers, pulled down and secured as a throat "hackle"

Tying sequence:

1. Tie in the thread in back of the hook eye, and clip any excess.
2. Wrap lead wire around the hook shank, the size of the lead wire based on the hook size and desired fishing depth. Clip any excess.
3. Spiral wrap the thread up and down the hook shank to secure the lead wire, ending up at the bend of the hook.
4. Tie in a bundle of ringneck pheasant tail fibers, and clip any excess.
5. Wrap the thread forward to just in back of the hook eye.
6. Wrap the bundle of pheasant tail fibers forward to a position about 1/4 back from the hook eye. Tie off, but do not clip any excess.
7. Use the thread to secure and position the remaining pheasant tail fibers under the body of the nymph as a throat.
8. Make a neat head, and tie off with a whip finish. Clip the excess thread.
9. Seal with head cement.

HEATHEN

This tiny midge emerger pattern has a post, which makes it visible on the surface despite its small size.

This small fly from Phil Camera is a midge emerger pattern, one that Phil says will work in 4 inches or 4 feet of water, fishing anywhere from top to bottom. Phil likes it best when fished right under the surface. While it was designed for and has been extensively fished in the Rocky Mountains, it is also a fly for any occasion when midges are in or on the water. In essence, the Heathen is sort of a Larva Lace version of a Serendipity, with a little body dubbing thrown in. It can be tied in any color, but this is the pattern and color that Phil finds the best under most conditions.

Tied by Phil Camera.

Materials Needed

Hook – Curved hook caddis or scud hook sizes 16 to 20
Thread – Black
UnderBody – One layer of pearl Krystal Flash
Body – Gray Larva Lace slipped over the underbody and segmented with the thread
Wing - White Larva Lace Dry Fly Foam or other foam post material
Thorax – Coarse hare's ear, dubbed in front and back of the wing

Tying sequence:

1. Tie in the thread in back of the hook eye and clip the excess.
2. Tie in the Krystal Flash facing forward and wrap the rest of the hook shank with the tying thread to the bend of the hook.
3. Wrap the Krystal Flash over the hook shank, stopping at the bend. Tie off and clip the excess.
4. Slip an appropriate length (one-half of the hook shank length) of Larva Lace over the eye and shank, sliding it back to the bend of the hook.
5. Wind a tapered wrap of tying thread in back of the Larva Lace and then spiral wrap the Larva Lace with the tying thread.
6. At the forward end of the Larva Lace, tie in a small piece of closed-cell foam. This should be about 1/3rd the way back from the hook eye.
7. Dub coarse hare's ear onto the waxed tying thread and wrap in back of and in front of the foam post to create a thorax.
8. Make a neat head, complete with a whip finish and clip the excess thread.
9. Seal the head with head cement.
10. Trim the post long for fishing as an emerger, or short to fish it as a nymph. (A tip here is to trim the posts of all ties long, then trim the fly shorter on the stream with nippers if you wish to fish deep.)

BREADCRUST

A simple basic nymph that is an old standard.

The Breadcrust is an all-purpose generic nymph that with the dark orange ribbed body and soft hackle is ideal to fish with a twitching retrieve from a downstream cast location. It is best in quiet pools, but with a short line can also be fished through pocket water.

Tied by Holly Flies.

Hook – Standard nymph hook, 1X to 2X long, sizes 8 to 14
Thread – Orange or brown
Body – Brownish orange fur, yarn or synthetic body material.
Ribbing – Stripped brown hackle stem
Hackle – Soft grizzly hackle

Tying sequence:

1. Tie in the thread at the midpoint on the hook shank, then clip the excess and wrap the thread to the hook bend.
2. Tie in the ribbing of a softened (soaked) stripped quill, then tie in the body material of brownish orange yarn or add dubbing this color to the waxed thread. Wrap the thread (dubbing) forward to a point in back of the hook eye, or wrap the thread forward followed by the body material or yarn. Clip the excess body material or remove excess dubbing.

3. Follow with the ribbing and tie off, then clip the excess.
4. Tie in a grizzly hackle by the butt, trim the excess and then wrap the hook shank with the hackle.
5. Tie off and trim the excess hackle.
6. Make a neat head, complete the fly with a whip finish and clip the excess thread.
7. Seal the head with head cement.

SPIRIT RIVER CADDIS PUPA

This imitates the stage of caddis life when they are in pupa form.

This is another caddis pupa imitation which recent fishing research increasingly has shown to be important as trout food. It can be fished at any depth, from right on the bottom with split shot on the leader to right under the surface with a lightly dressed leader. Two top colors are cream and green, with the cream shown here.

Tied by Spirit River.

Materials Needed

Hook – Scud shrimp style, sizes 12 through 18
Thread – Cream
Body – Caddis Cream Mottled Nymph Blend ™ or similar cream dubbing
Wings - Silver/black Wings & Things or similar clear or gray scud back material
Thorax – Peacock herl
Legs – Grouse or partridge

Tying sequence:

1. Tie in the thread at the bend of the hook, leaving a long tag end. Do not clip the excess.
2. Tie in the Wings & Things or other back material facing to the rear.
3. Add dubbing to the waxed tying thread and wrap the dubbing forward to a point about 1/3rd the shank length in back of the hook eye. Remove any excess dubbing.
4. Fold the back material over the dubbed body and secure with a spiral wrap of tying thread, up to the tie-down point. Cut the excess back material.
5. Tie in grouse or partridge fibers beard fashion.
6. Tie in peacock herl and wrap the thread to just in back of the hook eye.
7. Wrap the peacock herl forward and tie off, then clip the excess.
8. Make a small neat head, tie off with a whip finish and clip the excess thread.
9. Seal with head cement.

NEWBORN CADDIS

This is another of the increasingly popular caddis fly imitations available in recent years.

This fly from Spirit River is a tent-wing caddis pattern fished wet as a nymph. The transparent wings appear like the air bubble that surrounds caddis pupa as they rise to the surface, producing good solid hits. The Newborn Caddis can be tied in any color in addition to the tan described here, with other popular colors olive and gray. It is an ideal fly to fish when caddis are popping to the surface, since it can be fished at any level of the water column to take those trout not taking surface flies, or early in a hatch before the fish are rising regularly on the top. Fish it in a slow strip fashion, to simulate the motion of the natural as it rises from bottom to top.

Tied by Spirit River.

Materials Needed

Hook – Long shank nymph Daiichi 1560 or Maruto 7376 in sizes 14 and 16
Thread – Tan
Body – Light brown Angora dubbing
Wings – Swiss Straw
Antennae – Mallard flank dyed wood duck
Bead – 3/32-inch Black Brite beads

Tying sequence:

1. Bend down the hook barb and slide the bead onto the hook.
2. Place the hook in the vise, tie on thread, clip the excess thread and wrap back to the bend of the hook.
3. Add dubbing to waxed tying thread and wrap a tapered dubbed body to the hook shank midpoint.
4. Whip finish, clip thread and apply glue.
5. Slide bead back and jam over glue against the body.
6. Re-attach the thread in front of the bead and clip the excess.
7. Prepare Swiss Straw by making a wing about one-inch long, and half of the Swiss Straw width. Trim end to form wing shape.
8. Tie wing in front of the bead using a soft loop, with the wing evenly positioned around the bead.
9. Add dubbing to the waxed thread, wrap a thorax in front of the wing.
10. Tie down two dyed mallard flank fibers to angle over the wing.
11. Form a small head, whip finish and clip the excess thread.
12. Seal with head cement.

CDC EMERGER, OLIVE

The use of the fluffy and oily CDC feathers to float flies has become very popular in recent years.

This emerger takes advantage of the buoyant CDC feathers, along with a waterproof dubbing for the body. CDC stands for Cul De Canard, or French for the back end of a duck where oil glands make these feathers water resistant. Some research shows that it seems to be more the small air bubbles, captured in the fine filaments of the feathers, rather than the oil, that contributes mostly to the high flotation of these feathers. Also, it seems that once you have fished extensively with the fly, or especially caught a fish on it, it never reacts or floats as well the same way again. Any fly tied with CDC – and there are a lot of patterns and designs – is effective, but you might think about this before tying up a bunch.

Tied by Spirit River.

Hook – Standard scud style or Daiichi 1130 in sizes 18 and 20
Thread – Olive
Tail – Three to four fibers of olive saddle hackle
Body – Olive dubbing, Fine & Dry or similar
Ribbing – Pearl Crystal Splash, one strand
Thorax – Olive Fine & Dry Dubbing or similar product
Wing case – Dun CDC feathers
Legs – Dun CDC feathers

Tying sequence:

1. Tie in thread in mid-shank and clip excess.
2. Wrap to the bend of the hook and tie in the tail of a few fibers of olive hackle.
3. Tie in a single strand of pearl Crystal Splash
4. Wax the tying thread and add olive dubbing, then wrap the dubbing forward to a point 1/4 the shank length in back of the hook eye.
5. Remove any excess dubbing and wrap the strand of ribbing forward. Tie off and clip excess.

6. Tie in CDC feathers, with some under the body as a beard and some on top as a wing.
7. Add dubbing again to the thread and wrap forward to the hook eye. Remove any excess dubbing.
8. Make a neat head, complete with a whip finish and clip the excess thread.
9. Seal with head cement.

FLEDERMOUSE

This is a buggy-looking generic pattern that can imitate a sculpin or large nymph.

This fly, sometimes spelled Fledermaus, is a general suggestive nymph that is not designed to imitate any specific insect form but is close enough to a lot of them to work well. It is a good searching fly when you want to plumb the depths with a buggy looking offering. It can be tied a number of ways, including with or without a tail. The same basic design can also be tied in different colors to best imitate the nymphs on your home waters.

Tied by Chuck Edghill.

Materials Needed

Hook – Standard nymph hook, 2X or 3X long, in sizes 4 through 12
Thread – Tan or brown
Tail – Orange-brown Australian possum
Body – Blended dubbing in an orange-brown color, often muskrat, mink and rabbit. Synthetics in this color will also work well.
Collar – Orange-brown Australian possum
Wings – Barred teal or mallard, topped with brown widgeon or brown-dyed teal (optional)
Head – Peacock herl

Tying sequence:

1. Tie in the thread at the midpoint on the hook, then clip the excess.
2. Clip and tie in a small short bundle of possum for a tail.
3. Tie in the synthetic dubbing body material or mix the dubbing and apply to the waxed tying thread.
4. Wrap the dubbing forward, or wrap the thread forward, followed by the synthetic dubbing strand. Remove excess dubbing.
5. Prepare and tie in a collar of Australian possum, making sure that the material completely surrounds the hook shank and fly body.
6. Tie in wings of teal or mallard followed by a topping of darker brown teal fibers (optional).
7. Tie in peacock herl in front of the collar and wrap the thread forward to the eye.
8. Wrap the peacock herl forward and tie off.
9. Make a neat head, then tie off with a whip finish and clip the excess thread.
10. Seal with head cement.

COMPARAEMERGER

This is an example of a fly that combines the low-floating characteristics of a dun imitation with the emerging features of a surface nymph.

The Comparaemerger is sort of a Comparadun with a back-sloping wing so that it will more closely resemble those flies which have just struggled to the surface, rather than those that are in the early dun stage and better imitated by the original Comparadun. As with many of the Comparadun/emerger series, it can be tied in any size and any color desired to match the hatch on your local waters. The wing of deer body hair keeps the fly just barely floating in the surface film, which is a characteristic of natural emergers and part of the key to the success of this fly.

Tied by the author.

Hook – Standard dry fly or wet fly hook, sizes 8 to 16
Thread – Brown
Tail – Blue dun hackle fibers, divided and split
Body – Grayish brown fur dubbing or body material
Wing - Brownish gray deer body hair
Head – Butt ends of the wing, trimmed very short

Tying sequence:

1. Tie in the thread at the midpoint on the fly, then clip the excess thread.
2. Wrap the thread back to the bend of the hook and tie in the tail fibers. To divide the tail fibers, tie them down a little forward of where you would normally add a tail on a fly.
3. Tie in the body of dubbing on the waxed tying thread or tie in a length of body material.
4. Take one turn of dubbing around the hook shank in back of the tail, to allow dividing the tail fibers. If using body material, wrap the thread forward to the hook eye and then make one turn of the body material around the hook shank in back of the tail.
5. Wrap the dubbing forward and over the hook shank and the rest of the tail fibers, or wrap the standard body material forward and tie off with the thread in back of the hook eye. Clip any excess or remove excess dubbing.
6. Tie down a short prepared (clipped, combed, and stacked) bundle of deer body hair. This should be tied down so that the wing is slightly shorter than the hook shank length and tied in a down-wing position.
7. Make several turns to secure the wing, then wrap forward and under the protruding butts, make a small neat head and tie off with a whip finish.
8. Clip the thread and seal with head cement. Trim the butt ends of the wing short to make a head.
9. (An alternative to the above, is to clip the butt ends of the wing to form a head prior to finishing the fly. There is little danger of cutting the thread when doing this, since the thread hangs down and the wing is on top of the fly.)

DEEP SPARKLE PUPA

One of the first flies to imitate a caddis in the cocoon-like pupa stage.

The Deep Sparkle Pupa is a caddis fly pupa imitation designed by Gary LaFontaine. Caddis form a pupa after their cased larval form, sealing themselves into a sheath and developing legs and longer antennae. They are in these for a few weeks, then swim to the surface where they develop into the adult form which is imitated by the elk hair caddis and many other surface patterns. This pattern is particularly good, since it closely imitates both the insect and also the sheath in which it lives during this period of time, and in which it stays while struggling to the surface. It can be tied in many colors.

Tied by Spirit River.

Hook – Standard wet fly hook, in sizes 10 to 14
Thread – Yellow
Weight – Lead wire
Underbody – Green Antron yarn, wrapped or dubbed
Overbody – Green Antron yarn, pulled out and tied around fly as loose sheath
Legs – Grouse, woodcock or partridge fibers, tied in on sides
Head – Brown fur, dubbing or body material

Tying sequence:

1. Tie in the thread at the bend of the hook, then clip the excess.
2. Tie in a length of green Antron or other yarn, with a long tag end. Allow the tag end to hang.
3. Wrap the thread forward, to the 1/3rd-point on the hook shank, followed by the Antron yarn, and tie off the yarn. Clip any excess.
4. Comb out the tag end of the Antron yarn, separate it into two bunches (one each top and bottom or each side) and then pull the two bunches forward in a loose loop to make the sheath. Tie off and clip any excess yarn.

5. Tie in the legs, tying in one bundle at a time of the partridge or grouse, one short, small bundle on each side of the body.
6. Tie in a short length of brown yarn or add brown dubbing, wrap the thread (or dubbing) forward, followed by the brown yarn (if used) and tie off. Clip any yarn or remove any excess dubbing.
7. Complete the fly with a small neat head and a whip finish. Clip the excess thread.
8. Seal with head cement.

Steamers

MUDDLER MINNOW

This famous streamer pattern can be fished on the surface or down deep where it will imitate a sculpin or mad tom catfish.

The Muddler Minnow is one of those rare flies that, depending upon how it is tied and how it is fished, can be fished on the top, right on the bottom, or anyplace in the water column in between. Dressed with some fly dope, it is a great top-water fly, fishing in the surface film and twitching it along like an injured minnow. With its brownish coloration, it will also imitate bottom-living sculpins, and if weighted or fished with split shot on the leader, can be fished deep. Without weight or with no fly dressing, it can be fished in mid-depths. It is a great big-trout fly, and imitative of the one hundred-plus members of the sculpin family. It was developed about 1950 by Don Gapen, who designed it to imitate the plentiful sculpin found in the Nipigon River of Ontario.

Tied by Umpqua.

Hook – Standard streamer fly hook, 3X to 4X long, in sizes 2 - 12
Weight – Wrapped lead or non-lead wire, or no wire if fished on the surface
Thread – Brown
Tail – Mottled turkey quill fibers
Underwing - Gray squirrel tail
Body – Oval or flat gold tinsel
Overwing - Mottled turkey quill section
Collar – Natural brown deer hair, spun
Head – Natural brown deer hair, spun and clipped

Tying sequence:

1. Tie the thread on in back of the hook eye and clip any excess.
2. Wrap the hook shank with wire to weight, or leave unweighted if fishing the surface. Spiral wrap the lead up and down the shank with the tying thread.
3. Tie in the tail, then tie in the gold tinsel. Wrap the thread forward in tight even turns to a point about 1/3rd the shank length back from the hook eye. This thread wrap forms an even base for the tinsel body, and is a must if wrapping over wire.
4. Wrap the tinsel forward evenly, and tie off at the thread. Clip the excess.
5. Tie down a small bundle of gray squirrel tail, after clipping closely and combing out any body fur.
6. Clip matching quill sections from matched turkey wing feathers and tie down so that the wings act as a tent over the underwing. Position so that the wing extends no farther than the end of the tail. Clip any excess forward of the tie-down point.
7. Clip, remove the underfur and use an evener on a bundle of brown deer hair. Position it over the hook shank so that it is no longer than the bend of the hook. Hold the bundle in place and tie down with loose wraps of thread. The deer hair will flare as you pull the thread tight. Keep most of the deer hair on top of the hook shank, but allow some to spin around the hook.
8. If necessary, add another short bundle of natural deer hair to the first, taking two loops of thread around the bundle and hook shank and then pulling tight to flare the bundle. Make several wraps of the tying thread through the bundle to help secure and stabilize it.
9. Pull the hair back and wrap the thread around the hook shank, then complete with a whip finish and clip the excess thread.
10. Seal with head cement, then use scissors to trim the head into a bullet shape, leaving the deer hair tips flaring out and covering the wing.

BLACK-NOSE DACE

This basic streamer pattern is designed to imitate the color patterns of many of the small dace found in trout streams.

This is an Art Flick design from his classic book, *ART FLICK'S STREAMSIDE GUIDE,* which covers a few but very basic flies for trout waters. This was the only bucktail included in the book that concentrated on dries such as the Light Cahill, Quill Gordon, Green Drake and others. The design is changed here, since the original suggested polar bear, no longer available as a result of the threatened status of the bear and understandable U.S. trade restrictions. It is a good bucktail design that with the mix of hair color, can imitate a number of small trout stream baitfish.

Tied by Chuck Edghill.

Materials Needed

Hook – Streamer hook, sizes 4 through 10
Thread – Black
Tail – Red yarn, very short
Body – Medium silver tinsel
Wing - Layers of white bucktail, then black bucktail or bear, then brown bucktail, each about the same size bundle.

Tying sequence:

1. Tie in the thread in back of the hook eye, and clip any excess.
2. Tie in the tail at this point, long enough to extend in back of the hook bend.
3. Tie in the silver tinsel, and wrap the tinsel over the red yarn tail to the bend of the hook, then reverse to bring it back to the thread position. Tie off and clip any excess.
4. Clip the tail to proper length.
5. Prepare a bundle of white bucktail, remove the underfur and stack the hair in a hair evener to even the tips.

Position over the hook shank so that the wing is about 1-1/2 the length of the hook shank. Tie down and clip the excess.
6. Repeat the above with black bucktail or black bear.
7. Repeat the above with brown bucktail.
8. Make a neat, tapered head with the tying thread, then tie off with a whip finish. Clip the excess thread.
9. Seal with head cement.

MICKEY FINN

The bright colors of this old pattern have taken many trout, with particular effectiveness on brook trout.

Most trout fishermen have heard of this basic trout streamer fly that has been around since 1932 when writer John Alden Knight found it and his fishing group had phenomenal success with it on trout. It was originally named The Assassin by Knight, who did not invent but did popularize this streamer that was one of six color combination flies made by Wm. Mills Company. In 1936 it was renamed the Mickey Finn by Canadian war correspondent Gregory Clark, who named it for the knock-out drink that supposedly killed silent film star Rudolph Valentino. Even though less used today than some other more modern and popular patterns, it is still a knockout of a fly as a searching, early season streamer for big trout.

Tied by Umpqua.

Materials Needed

Hook – 4X to 6X long streamer hook in sizes 4 through 10
Thread – Black
Body – Flat silver tinsel
Rib – Oval silver tinsel
Wing - Layers of yellow, red and yellow bucktail

Tying sequence:

1. Tie in the thread just in back of the eye, and wrap tightly down to the bend of the hook.

2. Tie in a length of oval tinsel, with the tag end extending up to the eye of hook.

3. Tie in a length of flat tinsel, the tag end tapered to a long point. Alternatively, tie in with the tag end extending up to the eye of the hook.

4. Wrap tightly over the tinsel back up to just in back of the hook eye.

5. Wrap the flat tinsel tightly and evenly up to just in back of the hook eye and tie off. Clip any excess tinsel.

6. Use a spiral wrap to wrap the oval tinsel up to the thread position in back of the hook eye and tie off. Clip any excess tinsel.

7. Cut a small bundle of yellow bucktail, remove any underfur and place it in a hair evener to align the tips.

Measure the bundle to be about 1-1/4 the length of the hook shank and tie down on top of the hook shank. Clip any excess bucktail in front of the tie-down point.

8. Repeat the above with a same-size bundle of red bucktail.

9. Repeat the above again with a slightly thicker bundle of yellow bucktail. (Some tyers make all three bundles the same size, although the original pattern calls for the top yellow bundle to be about twice the bulk of either of the first two bundles.)

10. Finish by making a neat tapering head, and tie off with a whip finish.

11. Seal with head cement.

WHITE MARABOU STREAMER

Marabou streamers, as a result of their soft wing, have a lot of action in the water. They can be tied in any color.

This is a simple, almost generic streamer fly with a lot of action as a result of the marabou wing. While white is described here, it is also extremely effective in yellow and black, with the same simple tinsel body. Trout may take the black version as a leech or hellgrammite. Variations of this can include ribbing the body with oval silver tinsel (as with the Mickey Finn), adding a tag end of red yarn, and adding a topping of peacock herl. It can also be weighted if desired, using metal dumbbell eyes or metal beads or lead/non-lead wire on the hook shank before wrapping with tinsel. Because of the action of this fly, even when fished slowly and deep, it is an ideal early season big trout fly when fishing cold water when a trout's metabolism is still low and their movements are slow. The slim, minnow-like wavy action of the wing and the ability to keep it in the strike zone when weighted makes this a must for any early season box.

Tied by the author.

Hook – 2X to 6X long streamer hook in sizes 4 through 12
Thread - Black
Body – Flat silver tinsel
Wing - White marabou
Throat – Red calf tail

Tying sequence:

1. Tie in the thread just in back of the hook eye
2. Tie in a length of flat tinsel, the tag end tapered to a long point.
3. Wrap the tinsel to the hook bend, then reverse direction to bring the tinsel back up to just in back of the hook eye. Tie off and clip any excess tinsel. (If tying this with an oval tinsel ribbing and/or red tag end, then the directions and tying sequence will follow those of the Mickey Finn.)
4. Clip a length of marabou from the central stem, bundle it together and slightly moisten it for easier handling. Measure the wing to be about 1-1/2 times the length of the hook shank and tie down with several thread wraps. Clip any excess marabou forward of the tie.
5. Turn the hook over in the vise (point up) and prepare a throat of a small bundle of red calf tail. Clip from the body, comb out any underfur and position against the fly. The throat should be about 1/3rd to 1/2 the length of the hook shank. Tie in place with several thread wraps and clip any excess fur.
6. Turn the hook back over in the vise (point down) and make a neat tapered head with the tying thread. Tie off with a whip finish.
7. Seal with head cement.

EMERALD SHINER, THUNDER CREEK SERIES

This fold-back wing pattern of streamer resurrects an old New England style, and can be tied in many colors and designs.

This fly is unusual in that the bucktail body is tied forward of the fly, then folded back over the hook shank and tied back just far enough to form a head to the fly.It is one of a Thunder Creek series of streamer flies developed and popularized in the 1970s by Keith Fulsher. It is really an old style from the 1940s, developed and perfected by Carrie Stevens. It is innovative, in that it can be tied very thin, as did Fulsher, or thicker, as did Stevens. Fulsher ultimately developed ten of what he called "primary patterns" and five secondary patterns, all based on specific baitfish or baitfish families. This is one of the Thunder Creek series of flies, all of which vary, but all of which use the folded-over bucktail, bullet-head construction. This pattern is slightly changed from the original, which called for a body of emerald green tinsel or floss ribbed with medium embossed silver tinsel.

Tied by the author.

Hook – Standard streamer hook in sizes 4 through 12
Thread – White
Body – Pearlescent green Mylar tubing, slipped over the hook
Throat – White bucktail
Wing - Olive bucktail or brown bucktail dyed olive
Gills – Red paint over the white thread or red thread, lacquered
Eyes – Painted cream with black pupils

Tying sequence:

1. Cut a length of Mylar tubing and slip it over the hook shank. Tie in with white thread or light green thread at the rear, first tying down and then wrapping over the tubing end and securing with a whip finish. Cut the thread.

2. Tie in at the head end, in back of the hook eye, and secure the forward end of the Mylar tubing in place with tying thread. The thread should be just in back of the hook eye at this point.

3. Prepare a bundle of white bucktail, clipping close to the skin, removing the underfur and stacking in a hair evener.

4. Tie the bucktail by the butt to the under side of the hook shank, just in back of the hook eye, with the tips facing forward.

5. Prepare a slim bundle of olive or olive-brown bucktail as above, and tie in place, tips forward, on top of the hook shank.

6. Wrap the thread back to about 1/4 the shank length in back of the hook eye.

7. Fold the white bucktail under the fly, and the olive bucktail over the fly so that both are now in a standard streamer position and about 1-1/2 times the length of the hook shank.

8. Bring the thread up and over the two bundles of bucktail to tie them down with two loops of thread. Make sure that these are loose loops to retain the bucktail positions on the top and bottom of the fly. (An alternative way to do this is to fold one bundle over and tie down, followed by the second which is then tied down.)

9. Tie off with a narrow, neat whip finish and paint the thread with red paint. (An alternative to avoid painting is to tie off the bundles when the tips are forward, then switch to a bright red thread to tie down the bundles and make the red gills.)

10. Paint the eyes and pupils on the folded over head of bucktail, using a painting stick or two sizes of nail heads.

NINE-THREE

The Nine-Three is an old style of steamer that can still take a lot of trout.

This fly was named for the weight of the first fish taken on it – a 9-pound, 3-ounce landlocked salmon. The fly, originated in 1936 by J. Herbert Sanborn of Maine, is well known and excellent as a trout streamer. It, along with a host of other feather-wing streamers, is ideal as a big trout fly and for fishing any time of the year. As a result of the wing construction, it has a lot of movement and action in the water, although the wing does have a tendency to wrap around the hook bend. As with a lot of New England and Maine flies, some of which were early on used for trolling and to imitate smelt, it is tied on a very long-shank hook.

Tied by Chuck Edghill.

Materials Needed

Hook – Standard streamer hook 4X to 8X long, sizes 4 through 10
Thread – Black
Body – Silver tinsel
Wing - Sparse white bucktail, over which is tied two green hackles and then flanked by two black ones
Shoulder - Jungle cock (optional)

Tying sequence:

1. Tie in the thread at the head of the fly, just in back of the hook eye. Clip any excess thread.
2. Tie in a length of silver tinsel.
3. Wrap the tinsel to the bend of the hook and then reverse the wrap to tie off in back of the hook eye. Clip any excess tinsel.
4. Prepare, stack and comb out a thin bundle of white bucktail and tie in place so that it is no more than 1-1/2 times the length of the hook shank. Clip the excess butt ends.

5. Prepare two matched green saddle hackles and tie in place, then clip the butt ends.
6. Repeat the above with two black hackles and tie them so that they flank the green hackles. Clip the butt ends.
7. Tie in a pair of short jungle cock feathers, one on each side. Clip any forward excess.
8. Make a neat tapered head with the thread and then tie off with a whip finish. Clip the excess thread.
9. Seal the head with head cement.

GRAY GHOST

This most famous streamer has been eclipsed today by simpler styles, but is still a great minnow imitation.

The Gray Ghost is one of the classic streamers, and as with so many others, was developed in New England. It is a Carrie Stevens' design from 1937 and perhaps the most famous of the many flies that she developed over her long fly-tying career. It was also the fly on which she at one point caught a 6-pound, 13-ounce brook trout – a phenomenal catch, even for those earlier times. As with many flies of the period, it used jungle cock as a cheek. The originals varied in color of the wing, since Graydon R. Hilyard in his book *CARRIE STEVENS, MAKER OF RANGELEY FAVORITE TROUT AND SALMON FLIES*, notes that Carrie liked color in her flies, but was often limited by the materials available. The original dressing, which can be varied by availability of materials, follows.

Tied by Umpqua.

Materials Needed

Hook – A very long shank streamer fly hook such as the Partridge CS15 Carrie Stevens style 10X long heavy streamer hook, or Mustad 94720 8X long streamer hook

Thread – Black

Tag – Flat silver tinsel

Body – Orange floss

Ribbing – Flat silver tinsel

UnderWing - Four to six strands of peacock herl and white bucktail

Wing - Golden pheasant crest, then four gray hackles, all equal length

Throat – Golden pheasant crest

Shoulder – Silver pheasant body feather

Cheek – Jungle cock (optional, today)

Head – Black, with orange thread band in center

Tying sequence:

1. Tie in the thread at mid-shank, then wrap evenly to the bend of the hook and tie in the flat silver tinsel.
2. Evenly wrap the thread forward a few turns, followed by the tinsel, which is then tied off. Do not clip the tinsel.
3. Tie in the body of floss, then wrap the thread forward to a short distance in back of the head. Wrap the floss forward in an even tapered body and tie off.
4. Spiral wrap the tinsel forward and tie off, then clip the excess.
5. Tie in the white bucktail after preparing it, (clipping, combing, stacking and positioning). Add the peacock herl and tie off.
6. Tie in the golden pheasant crest, and clip the excess. Follow with two gray hackles, concave side in, on each side of the crest. Tie off and clip the butts of the feathers.
7. Tie in the throat of golden pheasant crest.
8. Tie in a shoulder of silver pheasant body feather on each side of the fly, tie off and clip the excess.
9. Tie in a jungle cock on each side of the shoulder, tie off and clip the excess.
10. Tie the head, at the same time tying in a short length of orange thread. Complete the head and make a whip finish to tie off.
11. Tie in a few turns of orange thread, and then tie off with a whip finish.
12. Clip and seal the head of the fly with head cement.

BLACK GHOST

Another of the hackle-wing style of streamer flies that imitate baitfish found in trout waters.

While Carrie Stevens of Maine was well-known for her New England streamers and for her Gray Ghost, the Black Ghost was originated in 1927 by Herb Welch of Mooselookmeguntic, ME. It is another of the well-known Northeast streamer flies where streamer fly-tying and fishing were, and still are, art forms. While the Black Ghost was originated as a pattern for landlocked salmon and brook trout (they call them squaretails), it has also proved excellent in the ensuing 75 years for trout on all waters.

Tied by Umpqua.

Hook – Long-shank streamer hook, 4X to 8X long, in sizes 4 through 12
Thread – Black
Tail – Yellow hackle fibers
Body – Black floss, wrapped heavily and tapered at both ends
Ribbing – Medium flat silver tinsel
Throat – Yellow hackle fibers
Wing - Four white saddle hackles, extending to the end of the tail
Cheeks – Jungle cock (optional today)

Tying sequence:

1. Tie in the thread at the midpoint of the hook shank, clip the excess and wrap to the bend of the hook.
2. Tie in the tail of yellow hackle fibers.
3. Tie in the tinsel ribbing, followed by tying down the black floss body material.
4. Wrap the thread forward to just in back of the hook eye.
5. Wrap the floss up and down the hook shank to build up a tapered body and tie off at the thread. Clip the excess floss.
6. Spiral wrap the tinsel up the body and tie off at the thread, then clip the excess tinsel.
7. Tie in a throat of yellow hackle fibers and clip the excess butt ends.
8. Choose and match two pairs of white saddle hackles, with the pairs concave side to the center, and tie down. Clip the butt ends.
9. Add a cheek of jungle cock to each side of the fly over the white wing, tying each feather in separately. Clip the butt ends.
10. Make a neat tapered head, then whip finish to complete the fly and clip the excess thread.
11. Seal with head cement. (Note: jungle cock is not used in the fly that is shown above, and is optional.

LITTLE BROOK TROUT

*The fact that trout are cannibalistic makes
this realistic imitation very effective.*

Sam Slaymaker, related to the lock company of
that name and a fine outdoor writer, developed this
as one of three streamers to resemble fingerling
rainbow trout, brown trout and as with this one,
brook trout. All are similar in design, and developed
after the theory that big trout are cannibalistic and
will eat young trout. This pattern, and the two
designed to imitate other trout fry, is less used today
than when developed several decades ago, but does
have a good record for taking big trout in waters
where trout fry and fingerling are found.

Tied by Pacific Fly Group.

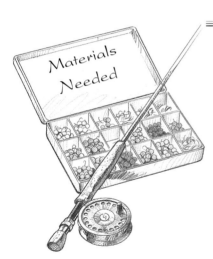

Materials Needed

Hook – Standard streamer fly hook, 4X to 6X long, in sizes 6 through
  12
Thread – Black
Tail – Sparse bright green bucktail, which is topped with strand of red
  floss.
Body – Cream spun fur
Ribbing – Flat silver tinsel
Throat – Sparse orange bucktail or hackle
Wing - Layering of sparse bucktail, white topped with orange topped
  with bright green, and a final topping of badger or squirrel tail
Cheeks – Jungle cock

Tying sequence:

1. Tie in the working thread at midpoint on the hook
   shank, clip the excess thread and then wrap to the bend
   of the hook.
2. Tie in a tail of bright green bucktail, after clipping,
   combing and stacking it. Top this with an equal length
   of red floss.
3. Tie in the flat silver ribbing, then a length of cream spun
   fur.
4. Wrap the thread forward to just in back of the hook eye.
5. Follow with the wrapping of spun fur, then tie off and
   clip the excess.
6. Follow again with the spiral wrap of tinsel, and tie off
   and clip the excess.
7. Tie in the throat of sparse orange bucktail after clipping,
   combing and stacking it.
8. Tie in a sparse wing of white bucktail after clipping,
   combing and stacking it.

9. Repeat the above with a sparse wing of orange bucktail.
10. Repeat the above with a sparse wing of bright green
   bucktail.
11. Repeat the above with a sparse wing of badger or
   squirrel tail.
12. Trim the excess wing material forward of the tie-down
   points.
13. Tie in a jungle cock feather on each side to form a
   cheek. Tie each one separately, and position parallel to
   the body.
14. Trim the forward part of the jungle cock.
15. Wrap a neat head of the working thread and tie off with
   a whip finish. Clip the excess thread.
16. Seal with head cement.

EDSON TIGER DARK

This bright attractor is ideal to use in deep trout pools.

Invented by William Edson for trout fishing in the New England area, this is one of two (the other is the Edson Tiger Light) that are basic attractor flies. This fly is similar to another old standard - the Warden's Worry, that also has a yellow body and tan/brown wing, but with the tail/throat colors reversed and the addition of a silver ribbing. Either of these flies are great, since yellow, along with white and black, seem to be basic colors for trout streamers, particularly in early spring.

Tied by the author.

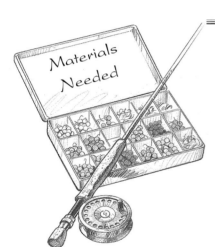

Materials Needed

Hook – Standard streamer hook, 4X to 6X long, in sizes 6 through 12
Thread – Yellow
Tag – Flat gold tinsel
Tail – Two yellow hackle tips
Body – Yellow chenille
Throat – Two red hackle tips
Wing - Tan bucktail or brown bucktail dyed lighter with yellow dye
Cheeks – Jungle cock (optional)

Tying sequence:

1. Tie in the thread at the midpoint of the hook, clip the excess and wrap to the bend of the hook.
2. Tie in the flat gold tinsel and wrap the thread forward three turns. Wrap the tinsel over the thread and tie, then clip the excess.
3. Tie in the tail of hackle tips, then tie in the chenille body material.
4. Wrap the thread forward to just in back of the hook eye.
5. Wrap the chenille forward and tie off with the thread, clip the excess chenille.
6. Tie in the throat on the underside of the body,.
7. Tie in the wing of brown bucktail, after clipping it closely, combing out the underfur and stacking in a hair evener. Clip the excess wing and throat.
8. Tie in the jungle cock cheeks very short (optional, today), tying one at a time on each side of the fly. Trim the excess butts.
9. Wrap to make a neat yellow head, then complete with a neat whip finish. Clip the excess thread.
10. Seal with head cement.

EDSON TIGER LIGHT

Peacock herl in the body of this fly makes it most attractive to trout.

Peacock herl has always seemed to be attractive to trout. Perhaps this is because it is a basic olive color – the color of many insects and baitfish, or perhaps it is because of the inherent sparkle and iridescence in the wrapped body material. In any case, it is the basis for this fly, which has reversed coloration in the wing and body of the Edson Tiger Dark. It is another New England streamer that is ideal on trout waters everywhere.

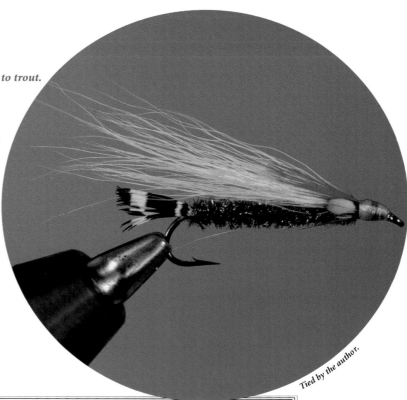

Tied by the author.

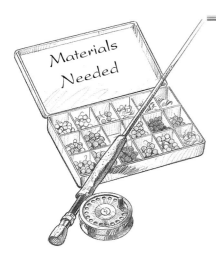

Materials Needed

Hook – Standard streamer hook, 4X to 6X long, sizes 6 to 12
Thread – Yellow
Tag – Flat gold tinsel
Tail – White tipped wood duck
Body – Peacock herl, twisted with black thread
Wing - Yellow bucktail, topped with red goose quill or flanked with two red hackle tips
Cheeks – Jungle cock (optional)

Tying sequence:

1. Tie in the thread at the midpoint of the hook, clip the excess and wrap to the bend of the hook.
2. Tie in the flat gold tinsel and wrap the thread forward three turns. Wrap the tinsel over the thread and tie, then clip the excess.
3. Tie in the tail of wood duck, then tie in a short length of black thread and several strands of peacock herl.
4. Wrap the tying thread forward to just in back of the hook eye.
5. Wrap the twisted thread/peacock herl forward and tie off with the thread, clip the excess peacock herl. (Alternatively, twist the working thread and peacock herl together and wrap forward, then tie off.)

6. Tie in the wing of yellow bucktail, after clipping it closely, combing out the underfur and stacking in a hair evener. Clip the excess wing.
7. Tie in a topping of red goose quill or flank the yellow bucktail with two hackle tips. Clip any excess material.
8. Tie in the jungle cock cheeks very short (optional, today), tying one at a time on each side of the fly. Trim the excess butts.
11. Wrap to make a neat yellow head, then complete with a neat whip finish. Clip the excess thread.
12. Seal with head cement.

SUPER STREAKER

Tied as a fly for trout in lakes, this basic Western pattern is simple to tie and has a lot of action in the water.

This is a pattern from the Pacific Northwest created by John Shewey. It is designed for lake fishing for trout, with the suggestion that a fast retrieve is best to entice hits. It is obviously an attractor pattern with the bright red marabou, and the marabou has lots of action in the water, particularly on the brief pauses when the marabou will flare out and act alive. While this one is in red, any color desired could be used to make this design a bright attractor fly, or one that has a duller and perhaps a more lifelike appearance of resembling a baitfish. The several tie-down points for the marabou make this a fly in which the wing is less likely to wrap around the hook bend, as might occur with a long marabou wing tied in only at the head.

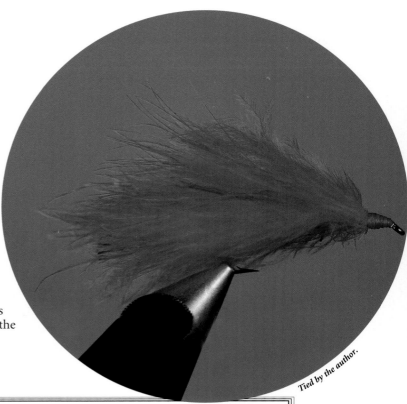

Tied by the author.

Materials Needed

Hook – Standard streamer hook, 4X to 6X long, in sizes 1/0 to 4
Thread - Red
Tail – Red marabou in which is mixed a few strands of red Flashabou
Wing - Two or three bundles of red marabou, tied in and spaced along on the hook shank to give the appearance of one long wing.

Tying sequence:

1. Tie in at the bend of the hook, and clip the excess thread.

2. Tie in the tail of marabou, followed by a few strands of red Flashabou.

3. Wrap the thread forward and tie in the first of the wings by tying down another bunch of red marabou.

4. Repeat as above, two or more times, to add more red marabou to form a complete wing along the hook shank.

5. Trim the butts of the forward marabou, then wrap a neat head with the thread and complete the fly with a whip finish. Clip the excess thread.

6. Seal with head cement.

CLOUSER MINNOW

This minnow imitation can be tied as desired to imitate the local minnows, and with it's dumbbell eyes, gets deep to where the trout are located.

The Clouser minnow, developed by smallmouth expert Bob Clouser, has become a fly-fishing classic in short order. While developed as a smallmouth fly, it is a natural for big trout also. Much of its success relies on the fact that with the heavy dumbbell eyes and slim profile, it gets right down to where the trout are located. It can be fished through riffles, in deep pools, in pocket water worked with short twitches or long even strips. Since it is tied with dumbbell eyes, it can be weighted using the smallest to the largest of the lead dumbbell eyes available. Just remember that the larger the eyes, the harder and more difficult it is to cast. Casting the heavy versions can come close to requiring the steelheader's "chuck-and-duck" method of fishing. Here is one of the many color combinations possible for this fly. Realize in tying this that the fly is fished with the point up, so that the throat is tied on what would otherwise be the top of the hook shank and the wing on the bottom to fill up the gap of the hook.

Tied by Umpqua.

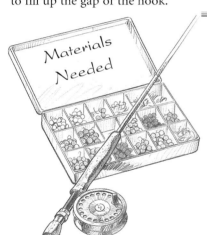

Materials Needed

Hook – Standard streamer hook, 2X or 3X long, turned down eye, sizes 4 to 12
Thread – Black
Throat – Orange dyed squirrel tail (optional)
Wing - Silver Krystal Flash mixed with white bucktail, then chartreuse bucktail
Eyes – Lead dumbbell eyes, painted red with black pupil

Tying sequence:

1. Place the hook in the vise normally (point down). Tie on the thread in back of the hook eye, and clip the excess.
2. Tie on the dumbbell eyes on the top of the hook shank in back of the hook eye.
3. Wrap down the hook shank past the dumbbell eyes and tie down a prepared (clipped, combed and stacked) small bundle of white bucktail. Trim the hair butt ends.
4. Turn the hook over in the vise so that the point is up. Tie in a small bunch of silver Krystal Flash, followed by a larger bunch of white, then chartreuse bucktail.
5. Trim the butt ends of these bunches, then wrap over them to form a head.
6. Complete the fly by making a whip finish, then clip the excess thread.
7. Seal with head cement.

ZONKER

Rabbit fur is another of the several soft natural materials that has a lot of action in the water. It makes this a very effective fly, particularly with a slow retrieve.

This fly, along with Matukas, is a big trout fly and essential for anyone fishing deep for large, cannibalistic trout. Designed by Dan Byford, it is a flashy fly as a result of the Mylar piping body and tail. It is like the Matuka in that the wing is tied down at both the head end and also at the bend of the hook. The lead can be left out to make an unweighted version or weight can be added with lead wire (instead of the metal sheeting), although you will lose the beer belly shape of the fly body. Since the pre-cut Zonker rabbit strips are readily available in a variety of colors, this is an easy fly to tie and an effective one to fish. Try it in black, brown and olive in addition to this basic original color. Since two threads and two tie-down points are used, you can use two bobbins or tie in the red thread and then half hitch it to secure it after tying down the body and before tying down the wing.

Tied by Chuck Edghill.

Hook – 6X long streamer hook in sizes 4 through 12
Thread – Black and red
Weight – Lead wire, alternatively metal self-adhesive sheet, cut to a pointed egg-shape and folded over the hook shank to form a beer belly shape.
Tail – Silver piping frayed out from the body tubing
Body – Silver Mylar piping
Wing - Natural white rabbit strip (Zonker Strip)

Tying sequence:

1. Tie down the thread, then wrap with lead wire. Spiral wrap the lead wire to secure it.
2. Tie down the red thread at the bend of the hook, and half hitch (if not using a bobbin).
3. Measure a length of silver Mylar tubing equal to a length of about 1-1/2 times that of the hook shank. Remove any inner core, and fray out the last 1/3rd of the tubing.
4. Slip the Mylar tubing over the hook and the lead wire, position the forward part in back of the hook eye and tie down the tail end with the red thread at the bend of the hook and the junction of the tubing and frayed tail. Half hitch it to secure it if not using a bobbin.
5. Push the forward part of the Mylar tubing back to be able to tie down the black thread in back of the hook eye.

6. Slide the Mylar piping forward and tie it off with the black thread.
7. Cut or use a Zonker strip that is about twice the length of the hook shank. Tie the strip in at the head of the fly.
8. Form a neat head to the fly and whip finish it to complete it. Clip the excess thread.
9. At the bend of the hook, open a gap in the rabbit fur at the thread location and make several wraps with the red thread to tie down the rabbit strip to the body and hook shank. Secure with a whip finish and clip the excess thread.
10. Seal the two wraps with head cement.

MATUKA, OLIVE

The style of tying this fly with the feather wing lashed to the body comes from New Zealand, and is very effective as a minnow imitation.

The Matuka is a New Zealand pattern that has found favor here as a big trout fly. As with the Zonker, the wing is secured to the body, although a feather wing is used in place of the rabbit in the Zonker. It is a simple fly, usually tied weighted to get it deep to where big trout live. As a result, it can be tied with a mono weed guard to prevent snagging, although trout flies are seldom tied this way. One advantage of this fly over other-feather wing streamers is that the hair wing will not wrap around the hook bend as a result of it being lashed in place on the body. It can be tied in any color, with black, brown, olive, white, yellow and spruce the most popular colors.

Tied by Brookside.

Hook – Streamer hook, 3X long hook in sizes 4 through 12

Weight – Lead or non-lead wire wrapped around hook shank

Thread – Olive

Rib – Copper wire or oval gold tinsel. (If using copper wire, it will add weight and might make the lead wire less necessary.)

Body – Olive or brown chenille

Gills – Red chenille or wool yarn (this is optional)

Wing - Olive dyed grizzly hen

Hackle – Olive dyed grizzly hen (also optional)

Tying sequence:

1. Tie in the thread at the head of the fly, then wrap the hook shank with tight turns of lead or non-lead wire.
2. Spiral wrap the wire with the tying thread, several times up and down the hook shank.
3. Return to the bend of the hook and tie in the ribbing wire or tinsel, followed by tying down the chenille.
4. Wrap the thread forward to a spot 1/4 the shank length in back of the eye on the hook shank.
5. Wrap the chenille forward, tie off and clip the excess. Tie down red chenille or red wool, then wrap the thread forward to just in back of the hook eye.
6. Wrap the red chenille forward to the thread, tie off and clip the excess.
7. Select four hen feathers, cupping two feathers on each side together and measuring so that the feathers are twice the length of the hook shank. Strip the excess

feather, tie down with the tying thread and clip the excess hackle stems.
8. Hold the wing parallel to the body, and pull the fibers forward so as to spiral wrap the ribbing around the body and wing without matting the feathers down.
9. Tie off the ribbing when reaching the head of the fly.
10. Choose a hen hackle, strip the soft end and tie into the fly. Clip the excess stem and then wind the hackle around as a wet fly collar hackle. Tie off and clip the excess hackle. (Note that this step is optional).
11. Finish by winding the thread through the hackle for additional reinforcement, then complete a neat head and tie off with a whip finish. Clip the remaining thread.
12. Seal with head cement.

MYLAR MINNOW

Simple minnow imitations of Mylar tubing are very effective and can be made in a variety of ways. This one has been painted to further enhance its life-like appearance.

Several people have come up with the idea of using Mylar tubing as the body and tail of the fly, to make a one-material fly. This is a simple variation of that in which a tail is added to the fly first and then the Mylar added to make the body. The fly can be finished with gills in red permanent marker and eyes in prism or paint added to make it a more realistic minnow imitation. Many will also use a black or blue permanent felt tip marker to darken the back of the Mylar body to make it more like a natural minnow with its camouflage shading. It can be easily tied weighted with a wrap of lead wire, but this is an unweighted version. While Mylar tubing is standard, this same fly can be tied in a more translucent form using materials such as E-Z Body, Corsair and similar translucent plastic tubing.

Tied by Umpqua.

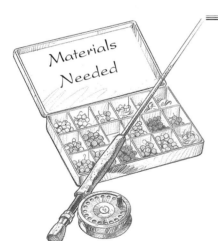

Hook – Standard streamer hook, 2X to 4X long, in sizes 4 through 12
Thread – Red
Tail – Light olive marabou, with a little silver Krystal Flash mixed in
Body – Mylar tubing

Tying sequence:

1. Tie the thread on the hook just forward of the hook bend and clip the excess thread.

2. Tie in a small bunch of olive marabou, followed by a few strands of silver Krystal Flash.

3. Wrap the thread forward up the hook shank to just in back of the hook eye.

4. Prepare a length of Mylar tubing about 1-1/2 times the shank length by removing the internal cord.

5. Place the end of the tubing over the hook shank so that the tubing extends to the right and tie down the end of the tubing just in back of the hook eye. When tied down, the hook will be exposed and the tubing extending to the right. Make sure that the thread wrapping the tubing in place is right against the back of the hook eye.

6. Wrap the thread back to the bend of the hook or previous tie down location.

7. Push the tubing back and over the hook shank, reversing it inside out.

8. With your left hand, position the tubing as you wish (fat or slim by adjusting the pull on the tubing) and then wrap over the end of the tubing with the red thread.

9. Secure with a few wraps, then make a whip finish and clip any excess thread.

10. Seal the thread with head cement and add eyes and gills as desired.

11. Eyes can be painted on using paint sticks or prism eyes can be added and then sealed with epoxy or head cement. Gills are easy with a red permanent felt tip marker.

SPRUCE FLY, LIGHT

A basic Western streamer fly that is tops in the Rocky Mountains.

Dave Hughes, in his writings, rates this fly as a top pattern for Rocky Mountain trout fishing. It even has the look of an excellent streamer for any trout waters, and in the light and dark versions can simulate a number of stream minnows and daces. The light spruce fly is featured here, with the dark spruce fly varying only with the substitution of a furnace hackle (dark brown) in place of the light-colored badger hackle wing.

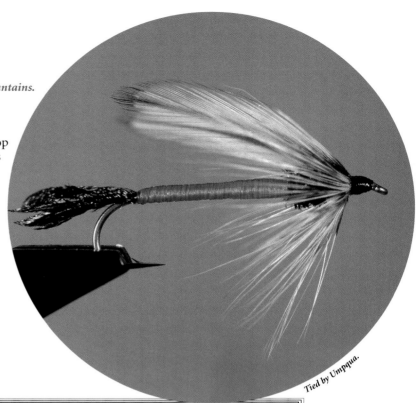

Tied by Umpqua.

Hook – 3X to 6X long streamer hook, sizes 4 through 12
Thread – Black
Tail – Peacock sword fibers
Body – Rear 2/3, red wool yarn; forward 1/3, peacock herl
Wing - Two badger hackles, tied flared (convex side together)
Hackle – Badger

Tying sequence:

1. Tie in the thread at the bend of the hook, clip the excess thread and then tie in three or four peacock sword fibers that extend about 1/2 the length of the hook shank.
2. Tie in red yarn at this point, with enough of a tag end to extend forward to just in back of the hook eye. Wrap the thread forward to the hook eye, then back to the 2/3 point on the hook shank.
3. Wrap the red yarn forward to the thread and tie off. Clip the excess yarn.
4. Tie in four to six peacock herl fibers, then twist them together with the tying thread for reinforcement. Wrap forward to just in back of the hook eye, strip off the excess herl and make several wraps to tie down.
5. Choose two matched badger hackle feathers, position them back-to-back and measure against the hook shank to about 1-1/2 times the shank length. Strip the excess fibers from the butt and tie the feathers in place. Clip the excess hackle stems.
6. Select a badger hackle, strip the butt end and tie in place in front of the wing.
7. Clip the excess butt stem and wind the hackle around the hook shank. Tie it off, clip the excess hackle and complete a small neat head with the tying thread.
8. Finish the fly with a whip finish and clip the excess thread.
9. Seal the fly head with head cement.

Terrestrials

McMURRAY ANT

The simple tying procedure and balsa wood floats in the abdomen and thorax make this an effective high-floater.

For some reason, trout seem to like the somewhat bitter, acidic (so I have been told) taste of ants. As a result, ant patterns have their place on both the limestone streams of the East and mountain streams everywhere. On these latter waters, ants will typically nest in rotten streamside logs and are frequently washed out and into the water during rain or any disruption of their nest. The McMurray Ant pattern can be tied in any color, since ants come in many colors. Typical patterns are black, red and cinnamon, but white is also possible as a termite imitation. All are ideal terrestrial trout patterns. As it is tied with the balsa wood abdomen and thorax sections, they are high floaters and ideal for those situations when trout are taking ants or other land-based insects. Ed Sutryn developed the original design. The component parts for making these flies are available through supply catalogs and fly shops.

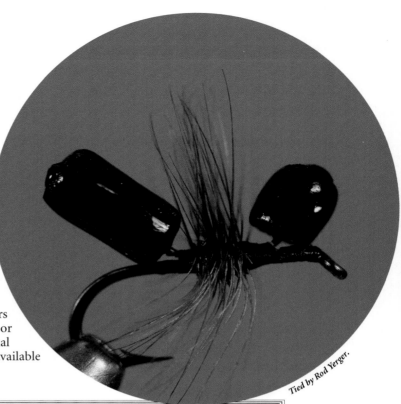

Tied by Rod Yerger.

Hook – Standard dry fly hook in sizes 12 through 20

Thread – Black to make a black ant as described here, thread color appropriate to the fly in making other color McMurray ants.

Body – Two small cylinders of balsa, the forward one slightly shorter and smaller than the rear section, both connected by a length of monofilament threaded through them. Painted appropriate to the ant pattern.

Hackle – Black, or a color appropriate to the pattern color

Tying sequence:

1. Tie in the thread at the center of the hook shank.
2. If not bought assembled, use a fine needle and fine monofilament to thread through short lengths of balsa cylinders, then paint them the desired color.
3. Tie down the prepared section of thorax/abdomen, with the mono curving up to give the abdomen and thorax a curved up appearance.
4. Tie in a hackle tip and clip the excess butt ends.
5. Wind the hackle around the waist of the fly, between the two balsa cylinders.
6. Tie off the hackle with thread and clip the excess hackle.
7. Hold the hackle out of the way and tie off with a whip finish. Alternatively, wrap the thread forward under the forward balsa body and then tie off on the plain hook shank.
8. Seal with head cement.

DEER HAIR INCHWORM

Inchworms are important summer trout food and easy imitations can be tied using green deer hair. This pattern has a tuft of red for surface visibility.

This inchworm is tied with light green-dyed deer hair or antelope hair. Only one material is used, other than the hook and thread, but that material must be spiral wrapped back and forth to make it retain the inchworm body form. It is an ideal fly for small stream fishing along the banks where inchworms occasionally fall into the water. Inchworms can be found in streamside trees and bushes from mid-spring through the summer. When they fall into streams trout eagerly gobble them up. There is never a "rise" or a "hatch" of inchworms, but when and where they are available, these offbeat flies are worth trying. Another easy way to make an arching (walking) inchworm is to use cylindrical foam slightly longer than the hook shank and tie down just the two ends of the foam to the two ends of the hook shank to make the inchworm appear to walk. The pattern here has the addition of the red yarn high-visibility marker.

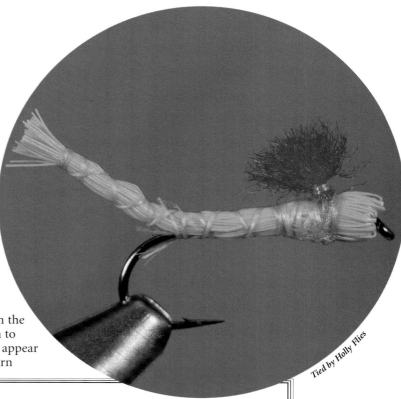

Tied by Holly Flies

Materials Needed

Hook – Dry fly hook 2X long in sizes 6 to 10, turned down eye
Thread – Light green or yellow
Body – Small bundle of light green or dark yellow deer hair
Visibility marker – Tuff of red yarn

Tying sequence:

1. Tie down the thread in back of the hook eye. Clip any excess thread.
2. Wrap the thread evenly and neatly to the bend of the hook, then back up to the hook eye. (This additional wrap to camouflage the hook shank is optional.)
3. Clip a small (large finishing nail size) bundle of deer hair, and comb out any underfur. Place it in a hair evener to even the tips.
4. Measure the deer hair bundle over the hook shank so that the bundle is about 1-1/2 times the length of the hook shank. Make a snug, but not tight, wrap to secure the bundle in back of the hook eye. About 1/4 of the hook shank length of deer hair should extend in back of the hook bend. (Since inchworms are blunt worms, you can clip the tip end of the hair bundle before doing this, then measure. Tapered or neat ends are not necessary for this fly.)
5. With the bundle in place, make a spiral wrap down the hook shank, wrapping snugly (but not tightly) around the hook shank and the bundle.
6. At the hook bend, continue this spiral wrap around the bundle alone that extends in back of the hook bend. (You may wish to reverse the hook position in the vise for this.) At the end of the bundle, reverse this to spiral back over the bundle, then over and up the hook shank and bundle to in back of the hook eye.
7. At this point, continue the spiral wrap over the forward part of the bundle that extends in front of the hook eye, then reverse this spiral wrap to return to the tie-down point.
8. In back of the hook eye, tie down a small tuff of red yarn on top of the deer hair, Wrap around the tuff so it stands upright.
9. Tie off with a whip finish, making snug (not tight) wraps. Clip any excess thread.
10. Seal the tie-down point with head cement. Alternatively, you can protect all of the thread with a seal of head cement over the whole fly.

LETORT HOPPER

Of the many hopper patterns available, this may be the most widely known. It has proven itself on all meadow and limestone waters.

Grasshoppers are common along meadow streams throughout the East and West. There are hundreds of species, details of which the trout and trout angler care little. The important thing is that they are a large and protein-rich trout food that can be easily imitated by a number of different patterns. Ernie Schwiebert developed the Letort Hopper, as a modified fly from earlier patterns of these large fun-to-fish flies. It is named for the Letort, a Pennsylvania limestone stream that was the laboratory for many writers. This isn't the only pattern for hoppers, and many can be found in books on terrestrial fishing. It is a good one however, and a hopper pattern should be in the fly box of all trout anglers.

Tied by Umpqua.

Materials Needed

Hook – Dry fly hook 2X long, sizes 6 through 12
Thread – Yellow
Body – Yellow fur dubbing or synthetic yellow dubbing
Wing - Brown mottled turkey feather, lacquered
Collar (or legs) – Tips of brown deer hair
Head – Trimmed deer hair

Tying sequence:

1. Tie in the thread at midpoint on the hook shank, clip the excess thread and wind it to the bend of the hook.
2. Tie in the synthetic dubbing or secure dubbing (natural or synthetic) to the waxed tying thread. Wrap the thread forward to a point about 1/3rd in back of the hook eye.
3. Wrap the dubbing forward to build up a body and tie off at the tying thread position. Clip or remove excess dubbing.
4. Cut a section of turkey tail or wing that has been previously lacquered or sprayed with clear sealer. Round off the free end with scissors. Position it tent-like over the wing so that the wing extends just beyond the hook and tie down at the head of the fly. Clip any excess turkey.

5. Select a bundle of natural deer hair, remove the underfur, even the tips in a stacker and position it so that it extends just beyond the wing. Tie down with two snug loops (not tight) of thread to hold the bundle on top of the wing, where it will flare up. Allow some of the hair to spin around the fly to simulate legs.
6. If necessary, pick another bundle of combed deer hair and add it to the first to make a tighter bundle. Clip the deer hair to a tight bundled head, leaving the long fibers to surround the fly and cover the wing. (Alternatively, to prevent cutting the working thread, finish the fly first and then trim. This is the method I prefer.)
7. Tie off with a whip finish in front of the hair bundle.
8. Seal the head and whip finish with head cement. Trim the fly if this has not yet been done.

LETORT CRICKET

This companion to the hopper is effective late in the trout season when crickets are more prevalent.

This simple but effective pattern is one of several cricket patterns, all of which will take trout. It was developed by Pennsylvanian Ed Shenk as a companion and variation of the earlier-developed Letort Hopper. While both were developed on a Pennsylvania limestone stream, both will work anywhere that trout will take hoppers or crickets or any larger terrestrial. As with the companion hopper, this imitation offers trout what looks like a large meal for easy taking.

Tied by Umpqua.

Materials Needed

Hook – Standard dry fly, sizes 8 to 12
Thread – Black
Body – Black fur or black synthetic dubbing
Wing - Black wing quill section
Collar – Tips of black deer hair
Head – Black deer hair, trimmed

Tying sequence:

1. Tie in the working thread about 1/3rd the shank length in back of the hook eye. Clip any excess thread.
2. Tie in a synthetic dubbing or yarn, or add black fur dubbing to the waxed tying thread.
3. Wrap the dubbing or body material to the bend of the hook and back up to the tie-down point again. Tie off and clip the excess or remove any excess dubbing.
4. Tie down a black wing quill section, using a soft loop to control the wing position. Trim any excess in front of the thread.
5. Tie in and stack a bundle of black deer hair, first preparing it (clipping, combing and stacking), and position the bundle with the tips to the rear to form the collar in the completed fly. Tie with a soft loop to keep the hair mostly on top of the hook.
6. Weave the thread through the head, then tie off in front of the head with a whip finish. Clip any excess thread.
7. Seal the head with head cement.
8. Trim the head (not the collar) with scissors or a new razor blade.

JASSID

This simple beetle pattern is suggestive of many beetles on which trout feed.

This was one of many seminal terrestrial patterns developed by Vince Marinaro and Charlie Fox during their trials and fishing on the limestone streams of south-central Pennsylvania. It represents beetles, aphids, small surface bugs and insects, and nothing in particular. It is an easy fly to tie if you have or can get the jungle cock nails, which are available, but which are expensive and in short supply. If you can't get these or don't want to pay their high cost, substitutes are available such as game bird feathers, coated with clear lacquer and cut to shape.

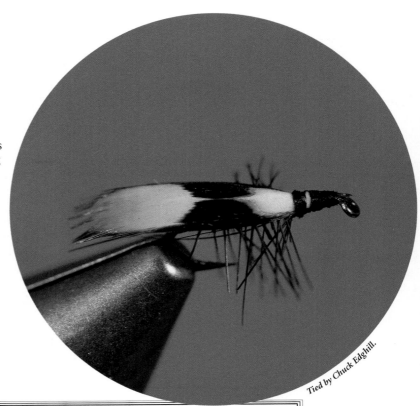

Tied by Chuck Edghill.

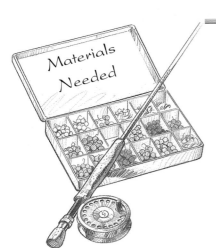

Materials Needed

Hook – Dry fly hooks, usually tied small on sizes 20 and 22 – can be tied larger on size 16 and 18
Thread – Black
Body – Black tying thread
Hackle – Black or other color as desired
Wing - Small jungle cock nail

Tying sequence:

1. Tie in the thread at the hook eye and wrap tightly to the bend of the hook. Clip off any excess thread.
2. Tie in the hackle, clip the excess butt ends and wrap the thread forward to the hook eye.
3. Spiral wrap (palmer) the hackle forward, then tie off with the tying thread and clip off any excess hackle.
4. Clip the hackle top and bottom so that the fibers extend out only from the side.
5. Tie down the single jungle cock feather, tying it flat rather than in plane with the hook. Clip any excess jungle cock.
6. Tie a small neat head and tie off with a whip finish.
7. Seal the head with head cement.

FOAM JAPANESE BEETLE

Foam beetles are simple to tie and can be tied in the shape of Japanese beetles or any other beetle.

Closed-cell foam, available through most fly-tying shops and also in sheet form through craft stores, is an ideal material for many floating flies and fly designs for trout and warmwater species. In cylinders and small "logs" it can be fashioned into McMurray Ants. Cylinder lengths of it can be used for dragonfly abdomens, and short plugs of it used for hopper and cricket bodies. This method of folding the foam over itself to make a beetle is one used by Bill Skilton and many others for terrestrial patterns of all types.

Tied by Riverborn Fly Company.

Materials Needed

Hook – Standard length to 2X long hook in sizes 6 to 10
Thread – Black
Body – Black foam, cut into teardrop or rectangular shape
Legs – Black hackle or black deer hair
Visibility marker – Tuff of red yarn

Tying sequence:

1. Tie in the thread in back of the hook eye, and clip any excess.
2. Wrap the thread tightly to the bend of the hook. Prepare a rectangular section of sheet foam, the length of the foam about 1-1/4 times the shank length and the foam width about 3/4 of the shank length. Tie in one end of the closed-cell foam, securing it tightly. Wrap the thread back up to a point about 1/3rd the shank length in back of the hook eye.
3. Tie in a hackle, make several wraps, tie off and clip the excess. Alternatively, clip a few (10-12) lengths of black deer hair and figure-8 wrap it into position so that the strands stick out of the sides like legs.
4. Fold the foam over and wrap it tightly at the thread position, taking care to avoid matting the legs with the thread. Tie in red yarn marker. Wrap the thread forward to just in back of the hook eye.
5. Use the thread to again capture the foam and secure it tightly to the hook shank.
6. Wrap the thread forward on the hook shank and tie off with a whip finish. Clip the excess thread.
7. Coat the head and the tie-down points with head cement.

RED ANT

Ants are important trout food and this wet style red ant is an effective and closely imitative pattern.

Unlike the McMurray Ant, which is a floater, this fly sinks and drifts with the current. Red is popular, though it can also be tied in black. Other useful variations are a brownish-red cinnamon ant and a black and red (red thorax and black abdomen). It can also be tied in white on a longer hook shank with a longer white abdomen to simulate a termite fallen from a rotten log along the stream bank. These ants are harder to follow when fishing, since they do not float on the surface as do most other terrestrials. A long rod/short line is best using a dapping technique that allows good control to the drift of the fly and the ability to react to the slightest strike.

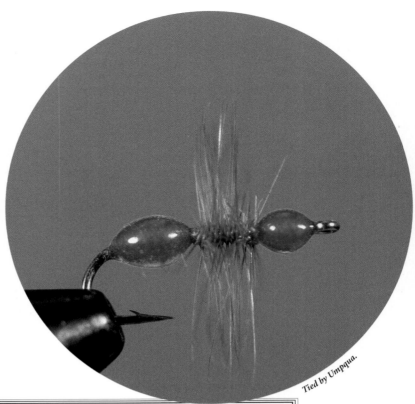

Tied by Umpqua.

Hook – Standard wet fly hook, 1X or 2X heavy hook, sizes 10 through 18

Thread – Red

Thorax – Light brown or brownish red floss

Abdomen – Light brown or brownish red floss

Hackle – Brown or ginger hen hackle

Tying sequence:

1. Tie in the thread at the bend of the hook and clip any excess thread.
2. Tie in floss and wrap the thread forward to the midpoint of the shank.
3. Wrap the floss back and forth to build up a neat tapered and rounded body or abdomen. Tie off and wrap slightly forward over the floss to preserve the thin waist of the fly.
4. Tie in a hackle and clip the excess from the butt area.
5. Wrap the hackle around the waist (midpoint of the shank) several times. (Since ants only have six legs, do not try to use the entire hackle fiber or make the fullest hackle possible.)Tie off the hackle with the tying thread and clip any excess hackle.
6. Wrap the thread forward to just in back of the eye.
7. Wrap the floss around the hook shank to build up a shorter and slightly smaller thorax of the ant forward of the hackle that simulates legs.
8. Clip any excess floss, make a small neat head and tie off with a whip finish. Clip excess thread.
9. Seal the abdomen, thorax, and head with head cement, taking care to avoid getting head cement on the hackle legs.

DAMSELFLY

Damselfly and dragonfly imitations are perhaps used more for bass, but are effective for trout. They can be tied using the parachute hackle suggested in the recipe, or using cut wings as shown here. The photo is slightly angled for the best view.

Damselflies are not standard dry flies, but they do float and do deserve a place in most trout fly boxes. They are best when fishing lakes, ponds, or slow-moving trout streams where damselflies are more prevalent than on small roiling mountain streams. Damselflies do offer a large chunk of meat for a surface-feeding trout, and thus are often taken with enthusiasm when presented on pools and long runs or glides. There are a number of ways to tie damselfly adults, including making bodies from deer hair, yarn, and other materials, but one of the best and simplest ways is to use long thin cylinders of foam, as per this Rainy Riding pattern. While this pattern uses cut wings tied spent-wing style, an alternative is to use parachute hackle or poly wing material to imitate the transparent, gossamer wings of the naturals. Note that the wings are out to the side as with the larger dragonflies, but the trout probably won't notice or care. While this pattern is for a blue damselfly, you can make them in any of the bright colors in which natural damselflies are found.

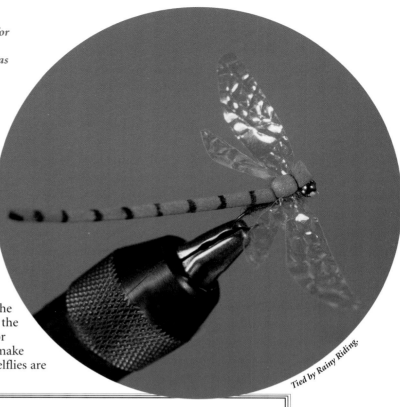

Tied by Rainy Riding

Hook – Standard dry fly hook in sizes 10 to 14
Thread – Blue
Tail – 3/64- or 1/16-inch diameter blue foam
Body – 1/8-inch diameter blue foam over dubbed blue body
Wings – Cut wings (parachute hackle is an alternative)
Eyes – Mono or Rainy's Bug Eyes

Tying sequence:

1. Tie in the thread at the midpoint of the hook and clip the excess.
2. Dub in some blue sparkle dubbing on the waxed tying thread and wrap this dubbing on the rear of the hook shank.
3. Prepare the length of tail foam by trimming the tail end to a point and cutting the tie-down end at an angle. Mark the foam with thin bands of black, using a fine tip permanent felt tip marker and rolling the foam on a paper towel as you make these concentric marks.
4. Tie the tail in front of the dubbed body and wrap over enough of the tail so that it will lie horizontal and parallel with the hook shank.
5. Cut the body foam cylinder in half lengthwise.
6. Tie in Bug Eyes on the front of the hook so that they will extend in front of the body once the fly is complete.
7. Tie down the cut wings or alternatively, tie in a long grizzly hackle fiber on a parachute post. Trim the butt end.
8. Wind the hackle around the parachute post and tie off, then clip the excess. (optional)
9. Add more dubbing to the waxed thread and add dubbing to the front of the hook shank.
10. Pull the parachute post over the body just wrapped, and tie down with tying thread after pushing the parachute hackle to the sides to make room. Make sure that the Bug Eyes are exposed and visible or adjust if necessary. (optional)
11. Whip finish to complete the fly and clip the excess thread.
12. Seal the wraps with head cement.

Miscellaneous

NEVERSINK SKATER

This simple skating type fly can produce explosive strikes.

This fly, developed as a skating, skittering type of dry fly, was developed by Edward Ringwood Hewitt and first written about by him in 1937. It remains a well-known and effective fly, though one less used than it probably should be. The fly, with its two (sometimes three) hackles, does not imitate in form or color any natural fly, but was developed to imitate the fluttering, jumping motion of butterflies touching the surface and sometimes - according to Hewitt - being ravaged by the trout. It is a neat fly, and one that is easy to tie, fun to cast and effective for taking surface feeding trout.

Tied by Chuck Edghill.

Materials Needed

Hook – Dry fly hook, sizes 14 and 16
Thread – Black
Hackle – Two large brown or black hackles

Tying sequence:

1. Tie in the thread at the midpoint on the hook. Clip any excess thread.
2. Tie in one of the hackles at this point so that when wrapped around the hook shank the concave side will face forward. Tie as compactly as possible, and tie off the hackle, clipping the excess. Use the thumb and fingernails of both hands to push the tie together to compact the hackle plane.
3. Tie in the second hackle just forward of the first, with the hackle this time tied so that the concave side faces rearward.
4. Tie off the hackle and clip the excess.
5. Again, use the thumb and fingernails of both hands to push the hackle ties together.
6. Tie off a tight whip finish, and clip the excess thread.
7. Seal with head cement.

MADAME X

Not a dry fly, but a high-floater, this Western fly is great for big trout.

The Madame X does float with the deer body hair tail, head and wing, but it is not really a traditional dry fly, and thus is placed in this miscellaneous category. It is a searching pattern for Western rivers and was developed by writer Doug Swisher for fishing the Bitterroot River in Montana. It is similar to the Ugly Rudamus, designed for the same river and type of fishing. It is sort of a hopper, sort of a water-strider, or perhaps could even be mistaken for a dragonfly, damselfly or stonefly when skittered on the surface. It can be fished with a skittering retrieve or with a dead drift through pools and riffles.

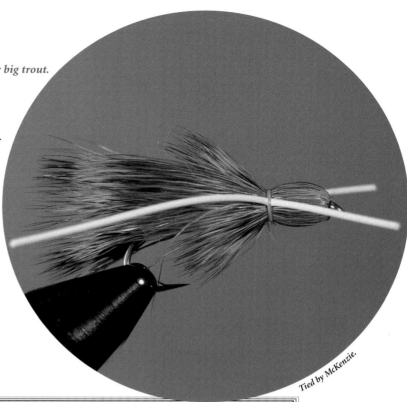

Tied by McKenzie.

Materials Needed

Hook – Standard dry fly, size 6 to 12
Thread – Orange
Tail – Natural deer body hair
Body – Fluorescent orange or yellow floss
Head and Wings – Natural deer body hair, tied forward and reversed over the body to form a bullet head and wings
Legs – White rubber hackle, tied in at the side

Tying sequence:

1. Tie in the thread at the midpoint on the hook shank, clip the excess and wrap the thread to the bend of the hook.
2. Tie in the tail of natural deer body hair, after first preparing it (clipping, combing and stacking it).
3. Tie in the floss body and wrap the thread forward to in back of the hook eye.
4. Wrap the floss forward over the butts of tail, then tie off at the thread position. Clip the excess thread.
5. Tie in the bundle of deer hair after preparing it, with the butts facing forward, this bundle must be long enough to fold back over the body with the tips reaching to about the end of the hook.
6. Wrap the thread back to a point about 1/3rd the shank length in back of the hook eye.
7. Fold the bundle of deer hair carefully back over and around the hook shank so that the tips face to the rear. With the thread in proper position, wrap the deer hair down so that the bundle now forms a bullet head and a surrounding deer hair wing.
8. After securing the deer hair, tie in two strands of white rubber/silicone leg material, one on each side and tied in one at a time. The legs should form an "X" and be equal in length in front of and in back of the tie-down point.
9. To complete the fly, make a whip finish, then clip the excess thread.
10. Seal with head cement.

HORNBERG

This fly can imitate a minnow as a streamer imitation, a salmon fly, or just be a generic buggy fly that trout attack.

This is one of those patterns, like the Muddler Minnow, that can be used dry or wet. Dressed with fly dressing and fished dry, the tented wing of mallard makes it resemble any of the many caddis flies. Without dressing and fished wet, it can imitate any of a number of baitfish and could be classed as a streamer. Seldom realized about trout flies is the fact that this fly, with the "dry fly style" hackle, will push water when fished as a streamer, and thus attract trout which feel these water pulses on their lateral line. This fact, more often noted about flies used for warmwater and saltwater fishing, might also account for its success and popularity on trout. It can also be tied with jungle cock cheeks.

Tied by Pacific Fly Group.

Materials Needed

Hook – Standard streamer hook, 2X to 4X long, 6 to 12
Thread – Black
Body – Flat silver tinsel
Wing - Dyed yellow calf tail flanked by two mallard flank feathers
Hackle – Brown and grizzly, tied as a dry fly hackle

Tying sequence:

1. Tie in the working thread about 1/4 of the shank back from the hook eye. Clip any excess thread.
2. Tie in silver tinsel, and wrap to the bend of the hook, then back again to the thread. Tie off and clip any excess tinsel.
3. Tie down a small bundle of calf tail after clipping it close to the skin and removing any underfur.
4. Prepare the two mallard flank feather wings, hold tent-like over the hook shank and tie down. Clip any excess forward of the tie-down point.
5. Tie in the two hackle feathers and clip any excess
6. Wrap the hackle feathers around the hook shank in the area between the wing tie-down point and the back of the hook eye. Tie off and clip any excess hackle.
7. Make a small neat head, complete with a whip finish and clip any excess thread.
8. Seal with head cement.

EGG-SUCKING LEECH

This fly imitates exactly what it sounds like – a leech feeding on trout and salmon eggs.

This fly, with the black body and red egg head, is designed to imitate a leech eating a trout, steelhead or salmon egg that has escaped from its redd and is tumbling downstream. It is an Alaskan pattern, then gained acceptance in the West and now is used almost universally on all trout streams. To simplify the fly, you can think of it as a woolly bugger with a red wrap of chenille added to the front end. For best results, fish it in a drift that will take it through deep pools and into quiet eddies. It has lead in this pattern to take it down, but can be tied without this for fishing shallower or with split shot on the leader in place of the lead in the fly. While shown in black with a red egg, it can also be tied with a body of any dark color and an egg of any bright fluorescent color. Pink is a popular egg color.

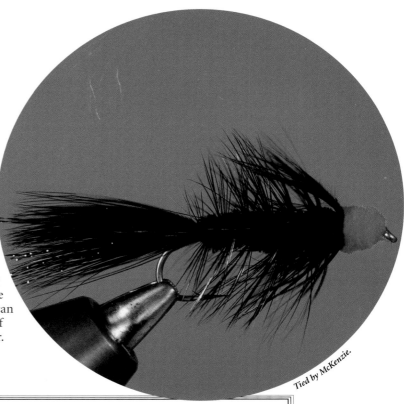

Tied by McKenzie.

Materials Needed

Hook – Standard streamer hook, 2x to 3x long, sizes 2 through 10
Thread – Black
Weight – Lead wire
Tail – Black marabou
Body – Black chenille
Hackle – Black, palmered over the body
Egg – Pink or red chenille

Tying sequence:

1. Tie in the thread at the rear of the hook shank and clip the excess.
2. Wrap lead around the body as desired. For an up/down action to the fly, tie it only at the front end.
3. Spiral wrap up and down the hook shank with the thread to secure and cover the lead wire.
4. Tie in the tail of marabou.
5. Tie in the palmering hackle by the tip end, then tie in the chenille body.
6. Wrap the thread forward to a point about 1/4 the shank length in back of the hook eye, or a spot leaving enough room to add an egg of red chenille.
7. Tie in a short length of red chenille, then wrap the chenille forward and then back again. Tie off with the working thread and clip any excess chenille.
8. Wrap the body chenille forward and tie off at the thread. Clip any excess.
9. Palmer wrap the hackle forward and tie off at the thread, after making a few final turns of hackle around the hook shank at the thread position.
10. Clip the excess hackle.
11. Seal with head cement.

SAN JUAN WORM

*Designed for the Western river of the same name,
this has been accepted as a basic fly for all waters.*

The San Juan Worm is the famous fly developed
for fishing the San Juan River in New Mexico. But it is
also useful anywhere there are trout. Numerous
worms live on the bottom of trout streams, often
small, but some larger than you would expect. In
addition, worms fall into creeks and streams during
rain and high waters where trout are actively
searching them out. And of course, worms are the
favored bait for early season spin-fishermen on those
waters that allow such fishing. The San Juan Worm is
the simplest of flies, and can be tied in any color
desired, although the red/orange/maroon colors are
usually favored as a result of their close resemblance to the
natural.

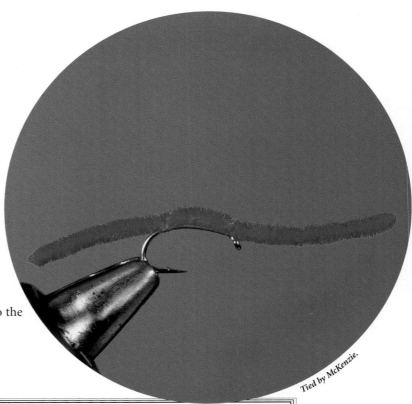

Tied by McKenzie.

Materials Needed

Hook – Any wet fly hook or a curved caddis larva hook in sizes 6
through 12

Thread – Red or orange, to match the worm color

Body – Vernille or Ultra Chenille in red, orange or maroon (other
colors also possible). Note that regular chenille will not work as well,
since the worm requires burning and tapering the chenille ends to
make it look more natural. (Whether the trout care or not is
something else!)

Tying sequence:

1. Secure the tying thread in back of the hook eye and
wrap evenly to the bend of the hook. Clip excess tag end
thread.

2. Tie down a length of Vernille or Ultra Chenille to
extend in back of the hook bend by 1 to 1-1/2 inches.

3. Wrap the thread forward to just in back of the eye of the
hook, making spaced wraps over the chenille as you do
so to secure it to the hook shank.

4. Tie off the thread in back of the hook eye using a whip
finish, tying on the bare hook shank under the forward
part of the chenille. Clip the excess thread.

5. Seal with head cement.

6. Use a cigarette lighter to gently singe each end of the
chenille, and use your fingers to roll the end to taper it.
(Take care to not burn yourself.) The flame will also
prevent the chenille from unraveling.

WOOLLY BUGGER

As a basic buggy fly, this pattern can imitate a leech, minnow, sculpin, or large nymph.

This is a searching or explorer fly, one that may and probably does imitate a lot of different things to trout. With the long marabou tail, and often-dark body, it might imitate a leech, hellgrammite, sculpin, small madtom catfish, and in small sizes, even some stonefly nymphs. It is a variation of the older Woolly Worm that is similar except for the short red yarn tail in place of the marabou. It is an ideal fly to use on new water, fan casting pools and spot casting riffles to find where the trout are located. You can continue this way with the Woolly Bugger or then switch to flies that might be more fun to fish, more of a challenge or even more productive. It can be tied in any color, using the same colors for body and tail or even contrasting colors in the tail. Typical colors that seem to be best for trout are black, gray, olive and brown. A variation of this basic pattern is to add some flash material such as Krystal Flash, Crystal Splash or Flashabou to the marabou tail.

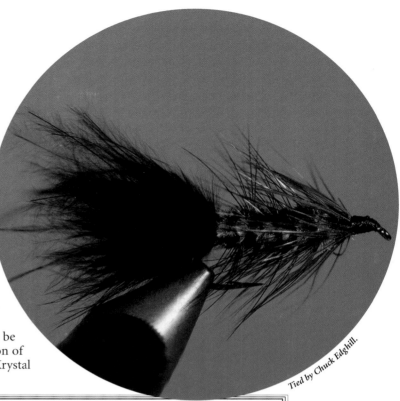

Tied by Chuck Edghill.

Materials Needed

Hook – Streamer hook, 2X to 4X long, in sizes 4 through 12
Weight – Optional – lead or non-lead wire wrapped around the body.
Thread – Color to match the fly color – black, gray, olive or brown
Tail – Marabou to match the fly color – black, gray, olive or brown
Body – Chenille to match the fly color – black, gray, olive or brown
Hackle – Soft, to give action to the fly, in colors to match the fly Body – black, gray, olive or brown.

Tying sequence:

1. Tie in thread at the bend of the hook shank.
2. If adding weight, wrap the lead or non-lead wire around the hook shank as desired. (Tie forward for a jigging action, along the entire hook shank for more weight.) Spiral wrap the thread up and down over the wire to secure it, and add a coating of head cement so that the wire will not bleed through and stain the body materials. Return the tying thread to the bend of the hook.
3. Tie in the marabou fibers. The tail should be about as long as the hook shank. Clip any excess fibers.
4. Tie in the palmering hackle by the tip end, then tie down the end of the chenille body. Wrap the thread forward to just in back of the eye.
5. Wrap the chenille forward in tight wraps over the hook shank or lead wire base. Tie the chenille off and clip any excess chenille.
6. Wrap the palmering hackle forward in a spiral wrap and tie off with the tying thread in back of the eye. Clip any excess hackle.
7. Wrap a neat head with the tying thread and tie off with a whip finish.
8. Seal with head cement.

GLO BUG

Trout do eat other trout eggs, and Glo Bugs are designed to imitate this food during the spawning period. Many different colors can be tied, along with bunches of several Glo Bugs on a hook or with the addition of hackle.

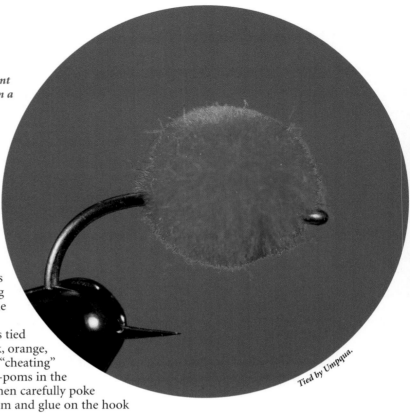

Tied by Umpqua.

The Glo Bug is one of those patterns that you have to have if you are fishing for steelhead, which of course are nothing more than West Coast sea-run Rainbow Trout, now however transplanted to many parts of the country. This fly is nothing more than a salmon egg imitation. It is simple to tie and ideal to use. Trout the world over are known for gobbling up eggs of their own and other species and this imitates a single drifting egg. Tie them in this, or any other, color and fish them with split shot to get the egg down deep. A variation of this is to use several bundles of the main color yarn, and one strand of a contrasting color to achieve an egg spot look. An easier way is to tie the Glo Bug you want, and then add a spot with an appropriate color permanent felt tip marker. This fly is tied bright red, but other colors are popular including pink, orange, yellow, white, cheese, salmon, flame, chartreuse, etc. A "cheating" way to make the same fly is to use bright colored pom-poms in the right size that are sold in all craft and sewing stores. Then carefully poke the hook point through the wire center of the pom-pom and glue on the hook shank with CA glue.

Materials Needed

Hook – Standard or stout wet fly hook in sizes 4 through 10
Thread – Bright red
Body – Bright red Glo Bug yarn

Tying sequence:

1. Tie the thread onto the hook at mid shank and clip the excess.
2. Tie in a short strand of Glo Bug yarn by the middle to the center of the hook shank.
3. Tie in one or more short strands of yarn to the hook shank at the same point.
4. Wrap the thread up the hook shank and tie off with a whip finish. Clip the excess thread.
5. Pull up the strands of yarn and clip them with scissors to make the Glo Bug a round egg shape. Make sure that you clip tight to preserve the gap of the hook, or clip close to the hook shank on the underside to maintain the hook gap.

Conclusion

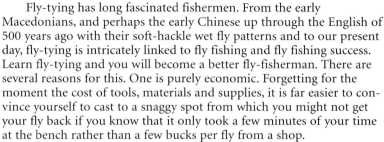

Fly-tying has long fascinated fishermen. From the early Macedonians, and perhaps the early Chinese up through the English of 500 years ago with their soft-hackle wet fly patterns and to our present day, fly-tying is intricately linked to fly fishing and fly fishing success. Learn fly-tying and you will become a better fly-fisherman. There are several reasons for this. One is purely economic. Forgetting for the moment the cost of tools, materials and supplies, it is far easier to convince yourself to cast to a snaggy spot from which you might not get your fly back if you know that it only took a few minutes of your time at the bench rather than a few bucks per fly from a shop.

Fly-tying also makes you more aware of how various materials work and look in the water and which materials with which flies might work best under certain fishing conditions. The fact that we tie imitations of mayflies, crane flies, caddis, stoneflies and other insects in nymphal, pupa and adult winged form also gives us a greater understanding of the food of the trout we seek. Couple that with the baitfish, leeches, terrestrials and other food — and our imitations of these — and we gain an encyclopedic knowledge (or we can if we apply ourselves) of trout habitat, ecology, biology, food and feeding habits.

We learn more about the water conditions under which aquatic insects live, and how trout react to them to search them out for food by grubbing on the bottom or gulping on the top. Tying flies also gives us a greater understanding of what makes an effective fly, what materials should go into a floating fly and what should be done to make one rapidly sink. This constantly developing knowledge also helps when fishing strange locations where we might have to visit a local shop and buy a few flies for local conditions to back up our basic boxes.

Fly-tying can be a hobby, a compulsion, an art, an education, and a science. It starts as a hobby, and can become a compulsion. It mirrors art when you design your own patterns and care deeply about how they will look in addition to how they will catch fish. It has the base elements of a science when dealing with the qualities and properties of materials used and the entomology of the insects studied to copy and fool trout.

Fly-tying is what you make of it, and as with a lot of things in life, you and your fishing life get from it what you put into it. There is a lot more to learn and any fly-tyer of any experience will tell you that he or she is constantly trying new techniques, perfecting old techniques, exploring new ways to tie and expanding their imagination in fly-tying. This book covers the basics. From this, and especially from Chapter III – FLY-TYING METHODS - you will be able to tie many types of patterns, to perfect most techniques and to evolve steadily in your fly-tying experience and abilities. Here's to good times at the bench. Hopefully, your fly-tying will lead you to more fun on the stream as you catch more trout on flies that you have created from your own mind using a hook, some thread and a little bit of fluff.

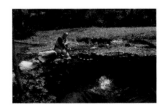

Boyd Pfeiffer

Bibliography

The following books are only a few of the many dozens available on fly-tying and trout flies. Rather than list an entire library of these books, those included here are designed to help with future fly-tying projects, to aid in learning or perfecting advanced techniques and always, suggesting more patterns of specific flies. They are all excellent and recommended for any reader interested in progressing in fly-tying after using this book as a base.

Borger, Gary. DESIGNING TROUT FLIES, Wausau, WI, Tomorrow River Press, 1991

Camera, Phil. FLY-TYING WITH SYNTHETICS – PATTERNS & TECHNIQUES, New York, NY, Voyager Press, 1992

Flick, Art. ART FLICK'S NEW STREAMSIDE GUIDE TO NATURALS AND THEIR IMITATIONS, New York, NY, Crown Publishers, 1969

Hughes, Dave. ESSENTIAL TROUT FLIES, Mechanicsburg, PA, The Stackpole Company, 2000

Huges, Dave. MATCHING MAYFLIES, Portland, OR, Frank Amato Publications Inc., 2001

Hughes, Dave. TROUT FLIES, THE TIER'S REFERENCE, Mechanicsburg, PA, The Stackpole Company, 1999

Knopp, Malcolm and Cormier, Robert. MAYFLIES, Helena, MT, Greycliff Publishing Company, 1997

LaFontaine, Gary. CADDISFLIES, New York, NY, The Lyons Press, 1981

LaFontaine, Gary. THE DRY FLY, Helena, MT, Greycliff Publishing Company, 1990

LaFontaine, Gary. TROUT FLIES – PROVEN PATTERNS, Helena, MT, Greycliff Publishing Company, 1993

Leeson, Ted and Schollmeyer, Jim. THE FLYTIER'S BENCHSIDE REFERENCE TO TECHNIQUES AND DRESSING STYLES, Portland, OR, Frank Amato Publications, Inc., 1998

Leiser, Eric. THE METZ BOOK OF HACKLE, New York, NY, The Lyons Press, 1987

Leiser, Eric. FLY-TYING MATERIALS, New York, NY, Crown Publishers, 1973

Linsenman, Bob and Galloup, Kelly. MODERN STREAMERS FOR TROPHY TROUT, Woodstock, VT, The Countryman Press, 1999

Martin, Darrel. FLY-TYING METHODS, New York, NY, The Lyons Press, 1987

Martin, Darrel, MICROPATTERNS – TYING & FISHING THE SMALL FLY, New York, NY, The Lyons Press, 1994

Miller, Bob, TRICOS, Allentown, PA, RodCrafters Press, 1997

Nemes, Sylvester. SOFT-HACKLED FLY IMITATIONS, Bozeman, MT, privately published, 1991

Richards, Carl; Swisher, Doug and Arbona, Fred. STONEFLIES, New York, NY, The Lyons Press, 1980

Schmidt, William E. HOOKS FOR THE FLY, Mechanicsburg, PA, Stackpole Books, 2000

Schollmeyer, Jim. NYMPH FLY-TYING TECHNIQUES, Portland, OR, Frank Amato Publications, Inc., 2001

Schwiebert, Ernest G. MATCHING THE HATCH, New York, NY, The MacMillan Company, 1955

Swisher, Doug, and Richards, Carl. EMERGERS, New York, NY, The Lyons Press, 1991

Talleur, Dick. MODERN FLY-TYING MATERIALS, New York, NY, The Lyons Press, 1995.

Veniard, John. FLY TYING PROBLEMS AND THEIR ANSWERS, New York, NY, Crown Publishers, 1972

Veniard, John. FLY DRESSING MATERIALS, New York, NY, Winchester Press, 1977

Index

Anatomy of a Fly

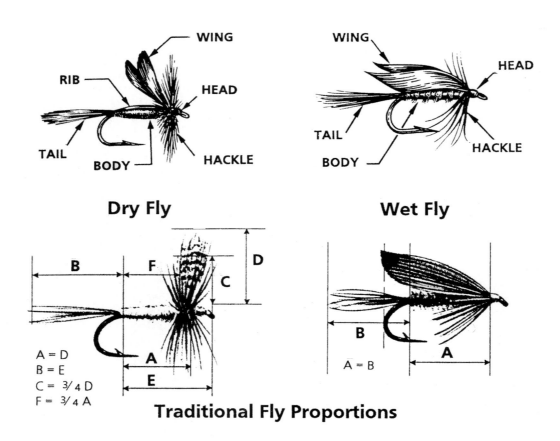

Dry Fly

Wet Fly

A = D
B = E
C = ¾ D
F = ¾ A

A = B

Traditional Fly Proportions

Black's 2001 Annual Buyer's Directory, Fly Fishing Edition, Black's Buyer's Directory. Used with permission.